"For all who aspire to great is the book for you. Caleb the bull's eye with basic relational behaviors and attitudes that nurture good relationships. Troublesome relationships don't need to bog down effective workflow and productivity. Put this book into the hand of every employee and reap a work culture of getting along at work. For those of you who learn through stories, Caleb tops off his book with three great stories that vividly illustrate and capture the heart."

Merle Herr
Resource Officer, Anabaptist Financial

"*Getting Along at Work* is written in an easy-to-read, easy-to-understand arrangement. It's applicable for both supervisors and employees; a good mixture of common sense saturated with Christian principles. Everyone will recognize some faults when reading, and the solutions for improvement."

Richard E. Shank

"Caleb Crider addresses one of the most overlooked cost centers in your company or organization—that of workplace strife. Boost morale and profits with this refreshing, practical, easy-to-read book on getting along at work, based on scriptural principles rather than humanistic philosophies. A must read for everyone in your organization."

Leland Ulrich
CEO of AFG Capital Group LLC

"Clear, insightful, and easy to read. Biblical, proverbial wisdom for the work place—or other places too."

Edwin R Eby
Bishop

"Caleb Crider has written a straightforward, no-nonsense human relations book charting the interaction skills we all need in everyday business."

Kenneth Burkholder
Sales

"We live in a world of conflict. Nations are at war, world leaders face tension, and church groups struggle to agree. But the struggle to get along isn't just *out there*. Conflict is often close to home. Countless people go to work each day struggling with difficult relationships in the workplace—relationships that are draining and that hinder effective work.

Whether you work on a construction crew, in an office, in the church, or on the foreign field, you will benefit from this Biblical, common sense approach to getting along with others. As Caleb observes, all too often the ball is in my court and a close look at myself is all it takes to transform a relationship from a burden to a blessing."

Weston Showalter

"*Getting Along at Work* provides inspiring, clear, and practical guidance that can better one's life, improve relationships, and honor God. I highly recommend it."

Anonymous church and business leader

Caleb's writing is clear, direct, and intensely practical. With plenty of examples and stories, he breaks a large subject down into easy, bite-size chunks.

Floyd Miller, employee at Anabaptist Financial

CALEB CRIDER

GETTING ALONG AT WORK

Work with others better.
Resolve relationship problems.
Become a respected coworker.

ENJOY YOUR WORK MORE.

© Carlisle Press September 2016
All rights reserved. No portion of this book may be reproduced by any means, electronic or mechanical, including photocopying, recording, or by any information storage retrieval system, without written permission of the copyright owner, except for the inclusion of brief quotations for a review.

ISBN: 978-1-933753-63-8

Cover design by: Jotham Yoder
Text design by: Lori Troyer
Printed in the USA by Carlisle Printing of Walnut Creek

2673 Township Road 421
Sugarcreek, Ohio 44681
800.852.4482

1-920162.5

Carlisle Press
WALNUT CREEK

Dedication

To all my great coworkers over the years at Faith Mission Home, Copeland Christian School, and Christian Light Publications. Thank you for enriching my life.

Table of Contents

Introduction VIII
Part 1: WORKING ON ME **1**
1. Find Your Inspiration 3
2. Have Realistic Expectations 11
3. Understand the Effort and Sacrifices 17
4. Take Responsibility for Your Relationships 23
5. Understand Spiritual Realities 29
6. Think Differently About Differences 33
7. Discover Your Blind Spots 39
8. Learn from Your Own Experts 45
9. Become a Professional 51
10. Put Humility to Work for You 59
11. Practice Not Getting Offended 67

Part 2: WORKING WITH OTHERS **71**

12. Apologize for Real 73
13. Improve Your Approachability 79
14. Say "Good Morning" to Your Coworkers 85
15. Communicate Courtesy and Encouragement 89
16. Compliment Your Coworkers 95
17. Put Yourself in Others' Shoes 99
18. Please Your Boss 103
19. Respect Your Coworkers 107
20. Stay Calm When Feeling Upset 113
21. Respond Peaceably to Attacks 117

Part 3: CASE STUDIES **123**

22. Daniel, the Godly Professional 125
23. Abraham Lincoln and His Cabinet 131
24. Thirty-Three Miners: Coworkers in Deep Trouble 137

Appendix 144
End Notes 145
Bibliography 146
Acknowledgments 148
About the Author 149

Introduction

If you have trouble getting along with others at work, I know exactly how you feel. After all, I'm the guy who threw a Skittle at a coworker—and it gave her a black eye. And I'm the one whose irritating comment caused a coworker to smack me with a book.

But my trouble getting along with people started long before that. I remember punching a fellow first grader in the stomach during recess at school. I said I had tagged her; she said I had not.

When I got my first job as a teenager, my people skills were not good. Conflict was normal, and sad to say, sometimes I even enjoyed it. Eventually—but not as soon as I should have—I became wiser.

I learned that not being able to get along with people was a burden and a liability. It brought stress and trouble to my life. By the grace of God, over time I took baby steps toward becoming a better coworker.

After I returned from vacation one time, a coworker (the same one who had hit me with the book) gave me a newspaper clipping as a friendly reminder of our acrimonious past. It was a Jon and Garfield comic, and Jon had just returned after an absence. "Did you miss me?" he asked Garfield. Garfield muttered to himself, "Yes, I did. In fact, I wasn't done missing you. Would you mind leaving again?"

You may have entertained similar thoughts about a coworker. Sometimes we wish certain people would walk out of our lives and never come back. Most of the time this is only wishful thinking. It is not going to happen, and often it wouldn't be good for us if it did.

I wrote this book because I needed this book. It represents my effort to learn how to get along with people at work. It is not professional counsel. Rather, it is common-sense advice—things I learned the hard way—that I believe will improve your ability to get along with the people in your workplace. This includes your boss and your coworkers, your customers, and your more occasional contacts.

Writer Samuel Johnson said, "People need to be reminded more often than they need to be instructed." Even if you know the basics of getting along with people, you will find fresh insights on being the kind of coworker that you would like to have. So take up this book as a reminder on one of the most important factors in your life and work—your relationships.

My goal is not to help you form deep, heart-to-heart relationships with your coworkers. Rather, I wrote *Getting Along at Work* with the vision of simply having relationships that work smoothly. My hope is that we will all learn how to navigate relationships at work in ways that bring less trouble, more fulfillment, and greater blessings to both us and our coworkers.

Getting Along at Work is divided into three parts:

Part 1 is foundational. It helps us see our coworkers in a completely new light and to think through our responsibilities in getting along with them. When we do our part, our relationships will improve.

Part 2 is practical. It focuses on ways we can proactively improve our work relationships and offers suggestions of specific things to do and say.

Part 3 is inspirational. It wraps up the book with three case studies of people who faced special challenges getting along with their coworkers. We can gain insight and motivation from Daniel, from President Abraham Lincoln, and from thirty-three Chilean coworkers who were trapped underground for sixty-nine days.

The "Take It to Work" questions at the end of each chapter help you get more out of the book by applying its principles to your own workplace and situation.

As any of my coworkers can attest, I don't always get along perfectly with them. I struggle with bad attitudes. I tire of the constant effort it takes for me to get along well with people. Though I still have lots to learn, the principles and concepts outlined in this book have made a tremendous difference in my relationships and responsibilities at work.

I believe you will benefit also.

Part One

Working on Me

Chapter One

Find Your Inspiration

As my wife and I walked into a restaurant in Mt. Hope, Ohio, with our three young children, a horse and buggy dashed past us in the parking lot. Stopping in surprise, we glimpsed an empty buggy seat—no one was inside!

The runaway horse and buggy crossed the parking lot, careened through a neighbor's lawn, and bumped across the sidewalk into the street on the other side. Hightailing recklessly through an intersection with head held high, it disappeared from our view.

I never found out what happened to the runaway, but I hope both the horse and all pedestrians and vehicles in the area escaped injury.

I had to think how people can be a little like the runaway horse. People who can't get along with others careen through life, wreaking havoc and leaving a trail of trouble behind them.

I have certainly done my share of bumping over the feelings of coworkers and recklessly causing them unnecessary distress. If you are like me, you could use a little help and inspiration in getting along with others at work. This is nothing to be ashamed of. Even the Apostle Paul once seemed to falter in this area.

Paul and Barnabas had been through a lot together, and had likely forged a close relationship. During the planning stage for another trip to visit churches they had helped start, they disagreed over which assistant to invite to go along. They each felt so strongly about it that they felt they could no longer work together. Paul and Barnabas got their way by going their separate ways, each with the assistant of his choice.

Inspiration makes the difference. Sometimes we have the inspiration to do something, but we aren't sure how to accomplish it. Other times we know how to accomplish something, but we don't have the inspiration.

When it comes to improving our "getting along skills," the inspiration, or the "why," comes first. Otherwise, we will never improve or learn what we should. Inspiration is why I can juggle (albeit awkwardly), but I cannot play the piano.

My mom wanted me to learn to play the piano. She enjoys playing hymns, and my siblings all learned to play. I didn't have the will or the "want to" to invest time and effort into piano practice, so I eventually gave up. I never advanced beyond pecking out a tune one or two notes at a time.

One skill I was inspired to learn was juggling. Someone showed me the basics of getting started (the best way is to learn how to correctly toss *one* object). Learning to juggle wasn't easy. At first I used tennis balls. They worked well except that they rolled away when I dropped them, which was often.

Soon I learned to practice beside my bed, so the balls wouldn't fall all the way to the floor. The only problem was that the bed got in the way as I lunged for wayward airborne balls. In the beginning balls usually headed away from me instead of sailing gracefully into my other hand like they were supposed to. When I did manage to throw them in the right direction, they collided in midair.

In spite of these difficulties, I persevered through each clumsy stage and finally mastered the simplest form of juggling. I'm not good at it, but years later, I can still juggle three objects. I am pleased with my achievement, but it only happened because I didn't give up. I had a "why."

Why we need inspiration. Improvement usually brings resistance. It's not easy to improve something. As grown-ups, we may forget how hard it is to learn something new. I recently helped my four-year-old learn to ride a bicycle without any training wheels. Balancing on two wheels isn't easy for a youngster accustomed to rolling along on four!

Improving our skills, whether it is business expertise, cooking abilities, or social graces, involves learning and doing something new. At some point, we are probably going to feel like giving up. We can get bogged down when things don't go like we wish or when we face skepticism from others.

Have you ever stopped in the middle of a project that wasn't going well and complained, "Why did I ever tackle this thing? This is crazy—I can't do it!" While writing this book, I sometimes thought, *Why am I doing this? Will this even help anyone? What right do I have to tell others what to do?*

Anytime we feel bogged down, it helps to remember our reason for tackling the project. Usually at the start we have an enthusiastic vision of what we want to accomplish. We are excited and optimistic. We can almost feel the satisfaction of successfully completing the project and achieving our goal. This is our "why"—the reason we began in the first place.

This initial enthusiasm often doesn't last long. However, at the core of that enthusiasm is the inspiration and vision for our efforts. Keeping sight of this "why" reminds us how essential it is to accomplish our goals and reinforces how important success is to us. It reminds us what we will lose if we give up.

Maintaining relationships at work is hard work, at least for me. I don't find it easy to consistently get along well with my coworkers, to smile and say "good morning," to graciously respond in difficult situations, or to sympathize with their difficulties. How do you find it?

If we aren't inspired to get along with others, we will not care enough about our relationships to work on improving them. We won't have a compelling vision or driving force.

At one time I didn't have enthusiasm for getting along well with my coworkers. I didn't have a "why" to remind me. I didn't have a vision that motivated me to work harder at handling conflict peacefully. So I didn't bother.

My employer said this about that stage in my life: "Sometimes you came across as boastful and with a spirit of superiority. Other times there was a lack of meekness and a desire to get along with others. You were confrontational and difficult-to-get-along-with with those you didn't mind having a poor relationship with." I didn't trouble myself with learning how to relate well to others, and therefore I brought trouble into my life.

As you consider your own situation at work, do you have a compelling vision that inspires you to get along with your coworkers? What are reasons we should work to improve our ability to get along with our coworkers, even though it is difficult? Here I'll offer you four:

1. Getting along well honors God. God did not make us to fight with each other. He made us to live in peace, as Adam and Eve did in the Garden of Eden before the Fall. Adam and Eve not only had a unique relationship with God, but they also had a wonderful relationship with each other. That was God's intention for all people. That Adam and Eve's oldest son became the world's first murderer is a powerful reminder that sin not only affected mankind's relationship with God, but it also affected our relationships with each other.

Seeking to get along well with others pleases God. The Bible urges Christians to avoid taking part in strife, but to "follow peace with all men" (Hebrews 12:14). God is honored when we display the fruit of the Spirit, including love, peace, longsuffering, and meekness. These qualities enable us to get along well with others.

First Peter 2:17 says, "Honour all men. Love the brotherhood. Fear God. Honour the king." When practiced with a sincere heart, each of these actions helps us follow Jesus' command to "love one another" and even to "love your enemies" (John 13:35; Matthew 5:44).

2. Getting along well blesses others. Did you know you have a big impact on how much your coworkers enjoy their jobs? Politics and conflict with coworkers or the boss are major reasons people quit their jobs. We have the ability to really ruin someone's day at work. More than once a coworker has gone home stressed out and frustrated with me.

Our coworkers appreciate when we make an effort to get along with them. The relationships we build with them enable us to serve them and be a blessing instead of a frustration.

We all know that customer service is important to any business, but so is "coworker service." Even if we work in operations far from the front lines of customer service, we have in-house customers. These could include the next person in the assembly line, our supervisor, or the people in the next department. All of these people are affected by our work, and they are blessed when we serve them well.

Doing our work well and keeping our attitude pleasant while going the extra mile to make our coworkers' work easier will help them have a much better day at work.

3. Getting along well blesses ourselves. God knew that Adam, though he lived in a perfect place, needed a "coworker." So God made Eve. We may not like to admit it, but we need other people. We couldn't have a relationship-free existence at work even if we wanted to. Learning to relate well to our coworkers not only blesses them, it also improves our own experiences at work.

I don't go to work to socialize, but relating to coworkers is an inherent part of my job. Not being able to get along with others will hinder my effectiveness and in the long run could jeopardize my job.

Good relationships at work enrich our lives. Even the perfect job would not be satisfying if we had no one with whom to share the load with, to depend on, to balance out our weaknesses, to help us solve problems, and to help us celebrate our successes and learn from our failures.

I hate stress. Conflict with others is frustrating and stressful, and it complicates our work and our lives. It can turn a good day into a bad day for people on both sides, and even third parties are affected. Collateral damage touches uninvolved coworkers, superiors, and even family at home.

If all of our work relationships were tense and frayed, we would dread going to work each day. By learning to enjoy being with our coworkers, we will make our work more enjoyable. This is a huge blessing.

4. Getting along well opens new doors of opportunity. To think about it another way, getting along well with others is good for our job security and improves our job prospects in the future. No boss is pleased when his people can't get along.

Employers prefer not to hire people who have a history of creating conflict. They know enthusiasm and mental energy that should be invested in important priorities are wasted in hostilities between coworkers. They value workers whose well-honed social skills enable them to get along with others.

One businessman said, "In addition to speaking to a prospective employee's supervisor, I always attempt to speak to individuals who worked with the applicant. I also attempt to contact neighbors who lived near the applicant. One bad apple can spoil the work environment for everyone. A bad report automatically rejects an applicant."

Another employer told me, "Getting along is a very basic skill that tells so much about a person. If he does not get along well with others, that is just the tip of the iceberg. This is a big reason not to hire. That is usually not a primary problem, but a symptom, and this will show up in their effectiveness in many other areas. In the interview, we subtly probe to figure out how well this person gets along with others."

Stanley Allyn observed, "The most useful person in the world today is the man or woman who knows how to get along with other people." The ability to build good working relationships with others makes us more valuable to our employers.

What would better relationships at work make possible for you? Consider these possibilities:
- Less stress and frustration
- More productivity and efficiency
- New friends
- More opportunities
- More fulfillment and enjoyment
- A promotion
- More trust and respect
- A pay raise

Like me, you may not consider yourself a people person, but people are a part of life. You and I are people. Our coworkers are people. Whether they are customers, a coworkers, or superiors, we will always need to deal with people, so we serve ourselves well by making it a priority to get better at it. The effort we put into relationships at work will be worth it.

If I can improve my relationships and become a better coworker, so can you. First, let's establish a clear "why" that we can come back to when we fail, lose focus, or get discouraged. This vision will inspire us in tough times and help give us determination to keep going when we feel like giving up.

TAKE IT TO WORK

1. Evaluate yourself. On a scale of 1 to 10, with 1 being very poor and 10 being excellent, how well do you relate with your coworkers?
2. Name your inhouse "customers" and describe how you serve each one. In what ways could you improve your service?
3. Imagine what it would be like to get along exceptionally well with each coworker. How would this change your experience at work? Does this picture excite and motivate you?

Chapter Two

Have Realistic Expectations

One summer before I was married, I traveled throughout the western states with three friends. On our list of things to do was a hike to the bottom of the Grand Canyon. Arriving at the canyon one afternoon, we made plans to start the next morning around five o'clock.

It was our first big hike of the trip, and I wasn't sure I could keep up with the others. We planned a grueling day—a hike down to the river in the bottom of the canyon and back to the rim the same day.

If we had any doubts about how exhausting our plan was, a sign near the canyon rim emphatically laid out the facts: "WARNING. Danger! Do not attempt to hike from the canyon rim to the river and back in one day. Each year hikers suffer serious illness or death from exhaustion."

At early dawn we passed the sign on the way down the trail. That afternoon, the four of us grouped around it again while a passerby snapped a celebratory picture. We were exhausted, but elated with our achievement.

Though we ignored its advice, the sign served an important purpose. It helped set our expectations and prepare us for reality. We knew in advance that the hike was grueling and tough, so we planned accordingly. With realistic expectations, we could prepare both physically and mentally to ensure we had the strength and fortitude to keep slogging on even when we were nearly worn out.

Realistic expectations are important when we set out to improve our relationships at work. Though we may have the vision for getting along better with our coworkers, rosy idealism won't get us far. It won't be long until we will run into a difficult situation we didn't expect—a coworker gives us a cold shoulder, or someone mocks our efforts or doubts our motives.

We will be far more likely to persevere and succeed in our new endeavor if we have realistic expectations up front. Here are some ideas that will help us stay firmly grounded in reality.

We shouldn't expect to get along well with everyone all the time. Even people who love each other dearly have occasional spats. Relationship problems are a part of life, so we can't expect anything otherwise from our relationships at work. We can expect to get along with certain people better than others, but even our closest friends at work will get on our nerves occasionally.

When a relationship with one of our coworkers starts to go south, there's no need to panic. Most likely it is part of the normal up-and-down pattern that relationships tend to follow. We should simply do what it takes to get things back on even keel again: make an apology, give a compliment, or allow a little time and space. Mistakes, misunderstandings, or moodiness are all temporary things that can be worked through.

We shouldn't expect to master all relationships by mastering one. Life would be easier if after building one successful relationship we would know exactly how to succeed in the next one. People being people, relationships will always be more complicated than that. Each person is complex, and their individual needs, habits, and background make them different from anyone else. Understanding how to relate to people means taking this into account and responding accordingly.

Successfully improving one relationship doesn't necessarily mean we'll be able to use the same approach in other relationships. Each person in our lives is unique, so when it comes to relationships, one size does not fit all. While strong relationships have many things in common—trust, respect, kindness—our approach to each relationship will need to be unique.

Be alert to how people respond to you, and adapt accordingly. For example, some people like to relate in a breezy, casual manner, but this approach may feel disrespectful if you approach them the same way. If you seem to be rubbing someone the wrong way, try to discern what you are doing wrong or how you may be misunderstanding them.

We shouldn't expect to get along with people the same way other people do. Sometimes I envy my friend Weston, who is sociable by nature. I marvel at how he seems to relate effortlessly to people. It would be useless for me to try to copy Weston's style or ways—it wouldn't be "me." My attempts would be forced and unnatural, and others would notice my pretense.

God made each of us different, and the way we connect with other people is different. A person can have a very reserved personality and still get along with people quite well even though he does not relate easily with others the way a more gregarious person might.

People's ways of relating to other people vary; that is normal. While we can learn a lot by watching other people, we shouldn't try to mimic them or judge ourselves by them. We should be genuinely ourselves.

We shouldn't expect everyone to like us all the time. In a perfect world, everyone would like us and respect us all the time. That is an unrealistic expectation. It is a selfish assumption to think that everyone needs to always understand and like us because we are reasonable, nice, or trying so hard.

If we try too hard to make someone like us, we risk coming across like an overexcited puppy that jumps up and puts his dirty paws on their clean clothes. It's impossible to force someone to like us, especially if they don't want to like us.

Not only should we not expect everyone to like us all the time, we should understand that we don't even have to be "friends" with everyone. Yes, our goal is to get along with everyone, but that doesn't mean we bring them to the same level of closeness that our good friends enjoy.

Some coworkers are simply acquaintances, and for them, a basic working relationship that gets the job done is sufficient. Of course, the more we like and enjoy our coworkers and vice versa, the more everyone benefits.

We shouldn't expect to have equally close relationships with all of our coworkers. We put a lot of effort into getting along with everyone, but does that mean we have to develop a close relationship with everyone equally? Do we have to enjoy being around one person as much as another? These are important questions.

In a situation where we find ourselves struggling to get along with someone, let me offer two strategies. First, we can ask God for a love like His for that person. The Bible asserts that "love is of God" (1 John 4:7) so it follows that He can place a divine love in my heart for a person who (to me, at least) seems unlovable. This kind of love enables us to be kind to others even when we don't particularly feel like it.

Second, we can begin noticing positive attributes about the person. When we do this, it helps move our focus away from the things that irritate us and helps improve our attitude toward the person. Taking this a step farther, we can mention the positive things we have noticed. For example, I could say things like, "I noticed how you handled that difficult situation with our boss yesterday," or "You helped me understand how to do my job better when I watched you do yours."

Different levels of relationship are to be expected, but we should treat each person fairly and respectfully whether we feel fond of them or not. When we actively dislike a coworker, our chances of being able to get along with him are doomed. Dislike tends to foster disrespect and distrust, which lead to open conflict.

We shouldn't expect to improve our relationships at work if our heart isn't in it. I once had a coworker I really disliked. He rubbed me the wrong way. Because my heart toward him was hard, for a while I wasn't really sure if I even wanted to improve my relationship with him.

When we find ourselves uncertain if we even *want* to get along with our coworkers, we won't be able to improve our relationships with them. Our hearts won't be in it; we won't have the commitment we need for the long haul.

This can cause other complications too. A coworker told me, "I once had a relationship I dropped because I didn't care about it until I realized that this was affecting others as well. I was creating a pattern of broken bridges."

Checking our attitude can be a diagnostic tool during times we aren't getting along well. Ask yourself, "Do I really want to get along better with this person, or am I half-hearted?" and, "Why do I feel this way?" When we waver, there is a reason for it, and we should examine our hearts to find the reason.

We shouldn't expect disagreements to automatically hurt our relationships. Getting along with our coworkers doesn't mean we never disagree with them, but it means we know how to handle disagreements.

I remember a committee meeting where disagreements resulted in some heated discussion. An observer stepping into the room may have been alarmed, but each committee member knew we were all on the same team, and we shared strong working relationships and commitment to a common goal. This enabled us to clearly express our positions and put the issue behind us when a decision was made.

Expecting to agree with someone all the time is unreasonable and unhealthy. As one person said, "If two men on the same job agree all the time, then one of them is useless. If they disagree all the time, then both are useless."

When coworkers know and understand each other well, their strong working relationship allows them to continue to get along even when they disagree. When we purpose to get along with a coworker, we can find common ground to agree on, and we can agree to peaceably disagree on other issues when necessary.

We shouldn't expect as much from others as we expect from ourselves. Generally, we expect our efforts in life to be rewarded. We expect a paycheck for our work, we expect juicy tomatoes as a result of tending our gardens, and we expect people to be nice to us if we are nice to them.

It can be depressing when we put a lot of effort into getting along better with a coworker and she acts as disinterested or uncaring as ever. We cannot do much about this except to consistently treat her as respectfully and carefully as we can.

This might not trouble us as much if we don't expect others to put as much effort into getting along as we do. We shouldn't expect others to always go the second mile, to always understand and encourage us, and to always sympathize with us. We should require more from ourselves than we expect from our coworkers. Their response may surprise us.

TAKE IT TO WORK

1. What are three things strong relationships have in common? Do you see them in your relationships at work?
2. Prioritize your relationships at work. Which ones are the most important as it relates to fulfilling your responsibilities well? Which ones need the most work?
3. Consider one relationship at work that you find disappointing. Why are you disappointed? Do you need to adjust your expectations? Can you change the way you treat the person?

Chapter Three

Understand the Effort and Sacrifices

One of my coworkers once saw a worker in a hospital cafeteria spill a three-gallon container of fresh coffee just before lunch. As the woman started to clean up the spill, she berated herself, calling herself a clumsy idiot.

This woman's coworker came calmly to her aid with a mop, saying, "This isn't so bad; we'll have it cleaned up in a jiffy." The smiling gentleness and prompt assistance of the second person soon quieted the frustration of the one who had spilled the coffee.

This helpful coworker is an outstanding example of the kind of person described in this poem found on an office wall:

Certain People Are a Joy to Know
People who know how to brighten a day
With heartwarming smiles and with kind words they say,
People who know how to gently impart
The comfort it takes to cheer someone's heart,

People who know how to always come through
When there's anything they can possibly do,
People who know how to willingly share,
Who know how to give and who know how to care,
Who know how to let all their warm feelings show . . .
Are people that others feel lucky to know.
- Amanda Bradley

This is not a simple to-do list. We can't become this kind of person automatically. This kind of person is a giver—the poem is really a list of things certain people give—and giving takes effort and sacrifice.

Getting along with people is the same as any other skill we want to learn: it takes work. Whether it is mountain-biking or flower-arranging or skeet-shooting, we will not excel in anything without investing time and effort.

Be willing to value relationships that work. How much effort are we willing to put into getting along with our coworkers? It depends on how much we prize strong working relationships.

If we want it to be, each relationship we have at work can be valuable in some way. If we understand the value of relationships, we'll be more willing to commit ourselves to creating and maintaining them.

Here are four ways relationships with coworkers can be valuable:

These relationships help us to grow personally and professionally. We learn a lot in both practical work skills and relational skills simply from interacting with and observing other people.

These relationships enable us to use our gifts and talents. Our abilities are gifts from God, and He expects us to use them to serve others.

These relationships allow us to find fulfillment as we help others. Connections with other people create opportunities for us to make a contribution to their lives while bringing meaning to our own.

These relationships help make our lives worthwhile. A self-centered life doesn't bring satisfaction, but an outward-looking focus that blesses other people brings meaning and purpose to life.

Yes, sometimes other people slow us down or complicate our lives. In times like these, we can remember this African proverb, a favorite quote of one of my coworkers: "If you want to go fast, go alone. If you want to go far, go together."

Be willing to invest in maintenance. One of my acquaintances ended up marrying one of her coworkers. Jennifer told me later that when her engagement was announced, an older coworker congratulated her and told her what a good man she was getting—that he was "nicer than you; he always has time to stop and talk."

Though the coworker felt bad and tried to explain herself, Jennifer knew what she meant, because it was true. Her future husband always took time to listen, while Jennifer usually avoided getting drawn into a conversation with this particular coworker who was known for talking on and on.

Getting along well with others requires sacrifice and investment. For example, it takes time—time to listen, time to care, time to encourage. Like the surface of my desk tends toward disorder, relationships tend to deteriorate unless they are maintained.

Samuel Butler once wrote, "Friendship is like money, easier made than kept." Relationships don't happen suddenly. They're a work in progress. Once started, they must be strengthened and maintained. They are always a work in progress.

Of course, at work, we can't spend all our time maintaining relationships, but if we dedicate every minute of the workday to our own projects without taking time to attend to our coworkers, our relationships will eventually disintegrate.

Be willing to put off selfish habits. Getting along with others requires us to rejoice with those who rejoice and to weep with those who weep (Romans 12:15). It requires us to prefer each other in honor and to "mind not high things, but condescend to men of low estate" (Romans 12:10, 16). It requires us to bless those who hurt us (Romans 12:14).

How does this work out in real life? Here are some things we will need to root out of our lives:

Pride. Proud people don't recognize their own glaring faults. They don't want to see other people get credit or recognition. If we have a spirit of humility, we will be able to apologize more genuinely, speak kinder words to others, and get along with people much more easily.

A critical spirit. It's not unusual for us to make small mistakes at work, and usually we catch and correct them right away without any problem. If we are in the habit of pointing out every little thing we think our coworkers did wrong, we make it hard for them to get along with us.

Wrong communication habits. Shouting. Interrupting. Sarcasm. Gossip. Backbiting. Communication is an essential part of every workplace, but it is easy to communicate in ways that tear down and discourage others.

Grudges and jealousy. Perhaps a coworker's action causes us extra work or he gets a promotion we wanted. Holding a grudge against that person is a sure way to hurt the relationship. Instead we need to give up grudges, forgive, and move on.

Demanding perfection. We cannot demand perfection from our coworkers. Every person has faults and flaws, so expecting perfect performance at work is unrealistic. If we are so demanding of others that they always feel like a failure, they will find it impossible to get along with us.

Getting offended. The opportunities to get offended at work are endless. Someone forgets to clue me in to an important piece of information. I wasn't invited to a meeting. I suspect someone doesn't like me. People who get along well with other people refuse to get offended easily.

Be willing to deal with the heart. If we consistently find ourselves doing the things on this list, we have a heart problem. I know from experience how conflict in my heart can hurt my relationships at work. When I am unsettled or torn different ways, I relate more poorly to others.

In *Getting Along with People God's Way,* John Coblentz writes, "Often when we grouch at others, when we are easily offended, when we reject one another, when we strike out and hurt, the person we really don't like is our sinful self. The people around us who peel away the layers of our masks and remind us of ourselves unfortunately get the brunt of our self-loathing."

Coblentz goes on to say, "If Christians are not nice (that is, if they are rude, selfish, proud, unfaithful, disloyal, judgmental, greedy, hurtful, and hard to get along with), they need to come to God along with everyone else. God changes people. Love for God produces love for people—real love, sacrificial, caring, and committed. God shatters our pride and selfishness, our 'me first' tendencies, and our down-the-nose arrogance."[1]

We will not grow without change in our lives. Change comes hard, but if we are serious about getting along with our coworkers, we must also be serious about coming to God and asking Him to change our hearts.

> **TAKE IT TO WORK**
> 1. List four reasons good relationships are valuable.
> 2. Identify one thing you need to sacrifice to improve a specific relationship at work.
> 3. Examine your heart. What is one selfish habit you need to deal with?

Chapter Four

Take Responsibility for Your Relationships

John Adams and Thomas Jefferson had a lot in common. They both worked on the Declaration of Independence. They both served as diplomats in Europe. They both served as vice president and president of the United States.

Though they were rivals from different political parties, Adams and Jefferson were friends. That is, until they weren't. They ran for the presidency against each other twice. The first time was in the election of 1796, when Adams won, and the second was in 1800, when Jefferson won. Adams retired from public office as the final strands of their frayed friendship snapped.

For twelve years neither man was willing to reach out to the other. The two former friends and former presidents didn't visit each other, and they didn't write letters. Neither one was willing to take responsibility for improving their relationship.

To be good at getting along, we must take responsibility for improving bad or borderline relationships. Our relationships aren't going to improve by themselves. A coworker likes to remind me, "If we do what we've always done, we will get the results we've always gotten."

One way to take responsibility for changing relationships is to change ourselves. Trying to "fix" the other person is often our first response, but that is not the right way. We need to take a look in the mirror.

Recognize the problem. People who don't understand or admit they have a problem getting along with others are some of the hardest people to get along with. To use one of Jesus' illustrations, sometimes they have a two-by-four in their eye while they complain about the speck in ours (see Matthew 7:3-5). We don't want to be that type of person.

The easy way out is to blame circumstances ("I was too busy"), our feelings ("I was having a bad day"), or the other person ("He was so unreasonable"). Blaming others doesn't acknowledge the role we must play in improving the relationship.

When I struggle to get along with a coworker, I have to realize that in some way I am part of the problem because I am involved in the situation. There are two of us, and I am one of them. Because I am in some way part of the problem, that means I can also be part of the solution.

Work on changing ourselves. If I were to ask you which person in your workplace needs the most growth or change, who would you name? Is there someone who immediately pops into your mind as someone who really has some issues?

Before you name the coworker who irritates you the most, consider that the Apostle Paul might have answered that question with, *"Me!"*

Paul seemed to think that of all the people he knew, he needed the most help. In 1 Timothy 1:15, Paul writes, "This is a faithful saying, and worthy of all acceptation, that Christ Jesus came into the world to save sinners; of whom *I am chief.*"

A businessman once told his people, "Personal accountability begins with YOU!" Perhaps he should have said, "Personal accountability begins with ME!" When we have Paul's attitude, we realize that we are responsible for ourselves—not for our coworkers. This principle of personal responsibility is expressed in a variation of the Serenity Prayer:

God, grant me the serenity to accept the people I cannot change,
The courage to change the one I can,
And the wisdom to know it's me.

We will never be able to force our coworkers to change the way they act or think toward us. We cannot make someone get along with us, but we can change ourselves. We control the way we act and think; therefore, we can change the way we think about and act toward our colleagues.

Changing the way we think about and relate to others at work is crucial. If people find it easier to get along with *us,* we will find it easier to get along with *them,* and vice versa. When we improve our own attitudes and actions, we are halfway toward our goal of a good relationship because of the positive impact this will have on our coworkers.

Make it easier for coworkers to change. By evaluating and changing our behavior, we make it easier for others to change theirs. Removing as many friction points as possible makes it easier for others to get along with us.

Saying that we cannot force a person to change does not mean we are powerless to influence them. Because our coworkers' responses to us are based largely on who we are (or who they perceive us to be), when we change who we are, our coworkers' attitudes and actions are likely to change over time.

What if we are just common laborers with no position and little respect? Can we actually make a difference? Yes, we can, because authority is not the same as influence. We don't have to be in a position of authority to be influential.

By changing ourselves we are making a small difference in our workplace because we are one dimension of our workplace. Our force for change is multiplied when our influence and example blesses, convicts, or inspires our coworkers to change themselves as well.

Fight off self-pity. Those of us with obvious relationship problems might look enviously at others who seem to breeze through life as friends with everyone. One friend who read a draft of this book before it was published told me, "I must say, books like this are a bit hard for me to connect with. Not because they aren't good, but for the most part I don't find it that difficult to get along with people." His experience has certainly been different from mine!

We may think people like this have some innate ability to avoid relational conflict, and that they have an advantage over the rest of us who have so many problems. This kind of thinking can be a way to avoid taking responsibility for our relationships.

Although some people are better at relationships than others, no one is born with the ability to get along effortlessly with others all the time. Even mild-tempered and easygoing people have relationship issues to deal with. Just ask one of them.

Once when I consulted my boss on a relationship problem, he told me about a similar problem he'd had with a person for years. I never thought about the fact that he would have difficult relationships to work through, but of course it made sense. Everyone has at least occasional "people problems," but some people have learned how to work with others in a way that reduces friction and confrontations.

Envy and self-pity are enemies of responsibility because they allow us to give ourselves a break when we really don't deserve one. They keep us from doing what we can do and what we should do.

Go first. For several years, a mutual friend urged John Adams and Thomas Jefferson to reconcile, and finally Adams wrote Jefferson a letter on New Year's Day 1812. Willing to renew the friendship now that Adams had taken the first step, Jefferson wrote back. The two retired presidents then corresponded frequently over the next fourteen years.

In an intriguing coincidence, these two founding fathers of America died on the same day—July 4, 1826. (All the more amazing because it was Independence Day.) John Adams' last words were reported to be "Jefferson survives," but Jefferson had died a few hours earlier the same day.

Though going first is the right thing to do, it doesn't guarantee success. Andrew Carnegie and his business partner-turned-enemy Henry Frick, two of the richest men of their time, didn't speak for almost twenty years after they had a falling out over business dealings.

As an old man, Carnegie sent a friend to personally deliver a handwritten letter asking Frick for a meeting to mend their relationship before he died. Frick replied, "Yes, you can tell Carnegie I'll meet him. Tell him I'll see him in hell, where we both are going." This kind of response is the sad result of unchecked bitterness.

John Adams' and Andrew Carnegie's example reminds us to be willing to go first when a relationship at work is stuck. Sometimes the other person may reach out to us first, but if they don't, we should be willing to go first. It's not likely we will receive as cold-hearted a response as Henry Frick's. Most often we will find that the other person is ready to meet us halfway.

Get started. Bad relationships drain our enthusiasm at work and bring a feeling of hopelessness. It's easy to feel like a failure and to think that the problem is too big or complicated to tackle even if we wanted to.

Changing bad relationships feels like a huge and impossible task, but getting started is easier than you think. Each of us lives in a web of relationships, and our world of work is a world of relationships. In addition to our own connections, other people's relationships are happening all around us.

We can start small just by paying attention to relationships and responses and what sort of things irritate people—ourselves included. This isn't hard.

By increasing our awareness of what is happening in relationships around us, we are equipping ourselves to better handle our own relationships. We will learn which habits and behaviors to cultivate and find out which ones to avoid. Make "get along with coworkers" part of your job description.

TAKE IT TO WORK

1. Who is responsible for the condition of your relationships at work?
2. To improve a relationship, which person must change first?
3. What are two ways you can change, or two friction points you can remove, to make it easier for your coworkers to get along with you?

Chapter Five

Understand Spiritual Realities

With its noise and dirt and sweat and businesslike atmosphere so different from a church service, you might think of your workplace as a distinctly unspiritual place. It may not be overtly spiritual in one sense, but regardless of its atmosphere, the things that happen in a workplace have spiritual implications.

Spiritual realities affect all people, even ungodly people. That is the way God made us. No one can get away from spiritual truths that govern the way things work in our experience.

Spiritual realities have a big impact on our relationships. Understanding the following four realities and adjusting our actions accordingly will greatly help us get along with our coworkers.

1. God loves everyone. God created each person you work with, and He loves each of them. Therefore, we go against this spiritual reality when we act like a certain coworker doesn't exist or we treat him disrespectfully or unkindly. In God's eyes we all have the same value.

In the book of Acts, Peter was accustomed to treating Gentiles as if they didn't matter to God. Then he learned that God is "no respecter of persons" (Acts 10:34), meaning that God doesn't respect one class of people more than another class.

God doesn't want us to treat others spitefully just because we don't like them or because they are different from us. Remembering that I am no more special to God than anyone else helps keep me from looking down on other people.

Whether we realize it or not, we have different levels of relationships with our coworkers. For example, some of my coworkers are close friends; others are more like acquaintances. In between are people I work with regularly and know well, but whom I don't trust with the same level of closeness as friends.

Having different levels of relationships is fine. It is even helpful in getting along with others. The problem is our tendency to peg a person's worth based on how much we like or dislike him.

2. Refusing to forgive is serious. Henry Ward Beecher said, "Every man should keep a fair-sized cemetery in which to bury the faults of his friends." Sometimes we can bury our coworkers' minor faults by simply choosing to overlook them, but when someone hurts us more deeply, a deeper response is necessary—forgiveness.

Forgiveness is an almost everyday part of getting along with people. It is essential to getting along. Forgiving others is part of maintaining spiritual life and following the example and teaching of Jesus.

Jesus made it clear that God will not forgive us if we do not forgive others (see Matthew 6:14, 15). God the Father grants us costly forgiveness through Jesus' blood, and Jesus modeled this kind of forgiveness on the cross by saying, "Father, forgive them, for they know not what they do" (Luke 23:34). An unknown poet wisely wrote:

> Respect the old when you are young
> Help the weak when you are strong
> Forgive the fault when you are wronged
> Because one day in life you will be old, or weak, or wrong. - *unknown*

In the last line, the poet predicts that "one day in life" we will be wrong. Actually, this "one day in life" will likely occur this week! None of us has a monopoly on the truth. I find that being wrong happens more often than I like to admit.

But when it comes to the matter of forgiveness, all of us were wrong in God's sight from the beginning. Now that we have experienced His gracious forgiveness, we are obligated to pass that forgiveness along to our coworkers when they wrong us.

Because it hurts our relationship with God and causes a root of bitterness to grow in us, refusing to forgive hurts us more than it hurts the other person.

3. Prayer changes things. We all know that prayer is powerful, but how often do we forget to use that power in our relationship problems at work?

When you realize that you dislike a coworker, take it as a sign that you need to pray about it. Pray for three things:

· *Pray for your own heart.* Ask God for a good attitude. Ask for special understanding of the other person's needs and for a soft heart.

· *Pray for your coworker.* Ask God to soften your coworker's heart toward you. As hard as it may be, ask God to bless his or her life. This simple act helps change your attitude.

· *Pray for the situation.* If there is conflict between you and your coworker, ask God to work out the details of the situation so it can be resolved peaceably.

Praying for our coworkers, especially coworkers we struggle with, works wonders. Our own efforts can't always bring resolution to relationship problems. Sometimes we need to pray and wait for God to work things out in ways we can't and in ways we don't expect.

4. Love is more powerful than hate. When someone hurts us or wrongs us, we are tempted to return fire and hurt them the same way they hurt us. The spiritual reality is that good is stronger than bad, right is stronger than wrong, and love is stronger than hate.

We can put this truth to work by returning good for evil like the Bible teaches. "Therefore if thine enemy hunger, feed him; if he thirst, give him drink: for in so doing thou shalt heap coals of fire on his head. Do not be overcome of evil, but overcome evil with good" (Romans 12:20, 21).

Hopefully we don't have outright enemies at work, but we can apply this verse to anyone whom we are having trouble getting along with whether or not they are openly antagonistic. We can put this spiritual reality to work by doing kind things for those who don't like us.

Repaying unkindness with unkindness—a shout with a snarl, a criticism with a snub, a curt remark with a disdaining look—weakens our position and doesn't show trust in the God who said, "I will repay" (Romans 12:19).

I remember a time when my relationship with one of my coworkers was a little rough. To show kindness and harness the power of love, I took a loaf of homemade bread to work. Another time it was freshly baked cookies. In addition to being acts of goodness, these gifts signaled that I wanted to do my part to help the relationship improve. And eventually, it did.

Even if the other person chooses not to respond to your kindness, you can have the satisfaction of knowing that you did all you could to heal the relationship. However, in most relationships, words and actions full of the power of love and goodness will win out in the long run.

TAKE IT TO WORK

1. List two ways understanding God's value system will change the way you relate to your coworkers, especially ones you dislike or tend to disrespect.
2. Say a prayer of blessing right now for a coworker whom you struggle to get along with. Can you make this a habit?
3. Are you holding a grudge against someone? Forgive them, and think of an action you can take to show your forgiveness.

Chapter Six

Think Differently About Differences

In romance, they say that opposites attract. I suppose that is true—my wife and I have very different personalities. Not only that, she is short and I am tall. In the workplace, differences often don't attract. They repel!

"Differentness" often causes friction between coworkers. You may have a reserved personality and work best in a quiet atmosphere where you can concentrate. A jolly colleague, however, may find that he can't think because "It's too quiet in here!" He'll whistle and hum and chuckle out loud—and irritate you without intending to.

We work with all kinds of people. Do you recognize any of your coworkers here? They may recognize you too.

The organized vs. the messy
The prompt vs. the procrastinator
The early bird vs. the latecomer
The risk-taker vs. the cautious
The serious vs. the carefree
The loud vs. the quiet
The smooth talker vs. the plainspoken
The gentle vs. the blunt

The slow thinker vs. the quick-witted

The leader vs. the follower

The toe-the-line type vs. the push-the-line type

The visionary vs. the practical

In addition to our differing personalities, we deal with differences resulting from our different ages, backgrounds, life goals, work experiences, and worldviews. These differences are very real, but do they automatically signal trouble for us? Let's look at four steps to follow when differences at work start to bother you.

1. Resolve to create new thought patterns. The way we think about other people affects the way we relate to them. If we actively dislike someone, even though we've never told him, the very presence of those thoughts will seep out, subtly influencing how we treat him and talk to him. "Out of the abundance of the heart, the mouth speaketh" (Matthew 12:34). My mouth has a habit of saying what my heart is thinking.

Changing our attitudes starts with changing the way we think, and changing the way we think makes it possible to change our actions. Our thoughts make a tremendous difference in our heart, and our actions spring from our heart. This creates a positive cycle: changing the way we think about others results in changed behavior; changed behavior helps cement our new way of thinking into a habit.

2. View differences as a positive instead of a negative. In many ways, diversity is valuable in a workplace. Asking, "What if everyone at work was just like me?" yields some eye-opening insights and helps give us a better perspective. If you are clashing with a colleague because the two of you are different, thinking through the implications of this question can transform your attitudes about that person. *What if this person was the same as me?* I am glad to be unique!

While it's true that differences can cause disputes, similar traits can also spark conflict. I am grateful that most people don't share my personality, skills, likes, and dislikes. If my coworkers were just like me, we would clash constantly. Imagine a workplace where each employee has a strong leadership trait or a similar personality. If everyone takes the lead, no one takes the lead. Both types are needed, or chaos will ensue.

Or maybe we can't stand being around a person who is overly aggressive and loves (a little too much) to get involved in new projects. No doubt this person has his faults, but imagine your workplace if everyone was just the opposite and hung back waiting for someone else to get the ball rolling. Nothing would ever get accomplished in such a workplace.

Differences are a positive thing; we can't let them make us uncomfortable. Different character traits, skills, and personalities bring a workplace to life. More than that, these differences are part of what makes organizations strong and flexible. Once we have learned to value diversity, we will have come a long way toward being able to get along with people.

3. Look for coworkers' strengths. Do we want our coworkers and superiors to focus on our weaknesses or our strengths? While weaknesses cannot always be ignored, I prefer that others appreciate and look for ways to use my strengths.

Instead of constantly complaining about our coworkers' weaknesses, we can look for their strengths. What do they enjoy doing at work? What do they excel in?

If all you can see is your coworkers' weaknesses, pick a weakness and examine its flip side. Just like "one man's trash is another man's treasure," the person you call "slow-witted" might be appreciated by others for being "thoughtful." You call the coworker who speaks his mind "blunt" or "harsh," but someone else may appreciate him as "a straight shooter."

What strengths might your irritating, overly talkative coworker have? What might she be contributing to the workplace that others are not? Does she do well at making new employees feel welcome? Perhaps she relates especially well to difficult customers.

Every weakness has an accompanying strength. If we can identify those strengths in our coworkers, we can deliberately dwell on those rather than letting their perceived weaknesses distract us.

4. Resolve to learn something from that person. Evaluate your own life in light of the strength you are trying to appreciate in your coworker. Ask, "Can I learn something from her to apply to my own life?"

Learning from coworkers is a way to honor them, especially if we tell them later how they have helped us grow and how much we appreciate them for it. Ralph Waldo Emerson said, "Every man I meet is in some way my superior; and in that I can learn of him."

We can learn both from our coworkers' strengths and their weaknesses or mistakes. Experience is a good teacher, but we are better off if we can learn the easy way—by watching someone else and learning from their experience.

The blessing of opposing digits. When you look at your hand, your thumb really stands out. It is noticeably different from your fingers in its location, shape, and size. More than that, the thumb has a reputation for awkwardness. Has anyone ever said that you were "all thumbs" at a certain task? That certainly is not intended as a compliment!

Yet who wants to live without thumbs? Without them our hands would lose important functions—grabbing, gripping, and squeezing.

A thumb is sometimes called the "opposing digit" because it is opposite the fingers. This pressure from the other side is what allows us to do all the amazing things we can do with our hands—just try picking up a small object without using your thumb.

We might have coworkers who appear to us to be thumbs: we think they are different, awkward, or less acceptable than other people. We may find them hard to get along with because they often oppose our ideas, and we butt heads. Maybe they just annoy us. However, like the thumb on your hand, these coworkers can serve a purpose if we let them. Perhaps they:

- Help us grasp ideas better as they present the opposing side.
- Enable us to see the bigger picture.
- Bring necessary balance to our zeal.
- Serve as examples of how *not* to do things!

In spite of the frustration we feel towards coworkers who are different from us, they can be blessings in disguise if we are willing to take the effort to appreciate them.

TAKE IT TO WORK

1. Compare yourself with a coworker you have trouble getting along with. Do different personalities cause the problem? How can the differences complement each other?
2. Think of a character trait that irritates you in a coworker, and then identify one way that trait could be an asset to your employer.
3. Based on your new understanding of differences, how will you respond the next time differences irritate you?

Chapter Seven

Discover Your Blind Spots

When I was younger I did some truck driving, hauling pallets in and out of factories. Driving a big rig was fun, but it's a job that requires constant alertness. I remember moving into the passing lane on the interstate and being surprised when a small car quickly scooted up in front of me. I hadn't checked my mirrors closely enough before changing lanes and had nearly pushed the car off the road.

Large trucks often have a sign on the back: "You're in my blind spot," or, "If you can't see my mirrors, I can't see you."

Truckers aren't the only people who have blind spots. Everyone does. Jesus knew how easy it is for us to see others' problems while being ignorant of our own. He warned us not to try to remove a speck from someone's eye when we have a big board protruding out of ours.

A blind spot can be a fault we have that we can't see or we ignore. We might be able to find these faults if we looked for them, but sometimes we don't even want to know about them. For example, we might characterize others' actions as worse than ours when in reality they were the same. We might say that someone else "demanded" something, while if we were describing ourselves, we would say that we "asked." Our terminology reveals our blind spot.

Another blind spot can be our ignorance of how we affect other people. It's much easier to see what others are doing to us than to see what we are doing to others. A blind spot is a little like bad breath—we are blissfully unaware of it, but others know it all too well.

What blind spot does this statement reveal? "People who think they know everything are very irritating to those of us who do."

The blind spot of similarities. When we are fighting with or getting irritated with someone at work, we typically blame it on our differences. *She thinks differently than I do, she is wrong, I am right, and that is why we are fighting.* Our logic says, "Why would there be a problem in the first place if we agreed?"

If we look beyond the surface of the situation, we might find the conflict is stemming from ways each of us are the same. I have found that if a coworker's attitude or action is irritating me, there is a good chance that I have the same problem. For example, I may think a coworker is acting overbearing, but he may have reason to think the same thing about me.

Consider two coworkers who don't get along very well. Whenever Ken makes a mistake or does something that inconveniences Paul, Paul loses control and rants against Ken.

Paul says, "I can't stand that Ken never admits it when he makes a mistake." He has a valid point—Ken sometimes avoids taking responsibility for his mistakes, and he hates when Paul blames him for something. Melissa, a perceptive colleague of the two, notices that Paul has a similar problem. He usually offers an excuse when things go wrong.

Similarities can lead to conflict. Paul and Ken are alike in many ways. They are both driven by the same need for top performance. They both hate to make mistakes, and both try hard to avoid them. Their pride leads them both to try to appear to be the best and to avoid being open about their mistakes. Their similarities have resulted in a sort of subconscious competition that sometimes brings open conflict.

If Melissa is brave, and if she is a good communicator, she could tell Paul and Ken why they are having trouble getting along. And if they are willing to listen and see their own blind spots, they can take steps to resolve their problems.

Other situations where conflict can result from sameness include relationships like these:

- A father and son or mother and daughter who share character traits or temperaments.
- Coworkers who are angling for the same position or assignment.
- Team members who want recognition or credit for a new idea or a completed project.
- Coworkers who are cultivating friendships with the same boss.
- People who try to appear the most intelligent or get the most attention.

Seeing ourselves as others see us. What can you do the next time you suspect "sameness" might be the culprit in a relationship struggle? First, honestly evaluate the situation to pinpoint what your coworker is doing that irritates you.

If her attitude is the problem (sometimes it is deeper than that), ask yourself if you have the same character trait or attitude. C.S. Lewis wrote about pride and self-conceit that "the more we have it in ourselves, the more we dislike it in others."[2] Or perhaps it's a coworker's habitual actions or words in response to circumstances that annoys us. Stop and examine yourself; often we can be guilty of doing the same things that irritate us when other people do them.

For example, I can become frustrated when coworkers don't respond promptly to my emails, especially when I am requesting something I consider a quick task or an easy question. Then I saw an unanswered email in my inbox one day and I realized that I sometimes do the same thing to other people. Sometimes I put off replying to emails. Although I may have started gathering the information or begun the requested action, my delay could be frustrating the sender because I had not acknowledged the note and informed them of my progress.

Poet Robert Burns got it right in the last stanza of his poem "To a Louse."

> And would some Power the small gift give us
> To see ourselves as others see us!

It would from many a blunder free us,
And foolish notion:
What airs in dress and gait would leave us,
And even devotion!

Discovering our blind spots helps us get along. If we have the same problem as the other person, then the problem must not be too bad! If we like ourselves the way we are, why can't we like it when other people are the same way?

More seriously, finding others' faults in ourselves helps us see ourselves as others see us. It brings our blind spots into plain view. If we are striving for excellence in relationships, it tells us where we need to improve.

Realizing we share attributes with our coworkers helps us find common ground. It reminds us we are not better than they are and helps humble us. Remembering that I probably irritate other people just as often as they irritate me helps me to be more gracious with them. After all, I want them to be gracious to me.

In the example above, realizing that I don't always send timely replies to emails keeps me from getting as frustrated when others don't respond to me. It also drives me to be more diligent in replying promptly to emails.

We cannot with integrity criticize someone else for a problem we are ignoring in our own life. It is like a black pot mocking a shiny kettle for being dirty.

"Oho!" said the pot to the kettle.
"You are dirty and ugly and black!
Sure no one would think you were metal,
Except when you're given a crack."

"Not so! not so!" kettle said to the pot;
"'Tis your own dirty image you see;
For I am so clean — without blemish or blot —
That your blackness is mirrored in me."

TAKE IT TO WORK

1. Analyze the terminology you typically use to describe your actions. Are you honest and objective? How can you improve?
2. How can you see yourself as your coworkers see you?
3. Is there a trait in a coworker that irritates you, but honest evaluation shows that you possess it also? What will you do to alleviate the irritation?

Chapter Eight

Learn from Your Own Experts

Do you subscribe to any trade magazines? Read industry newsletters? Attend conferences or seminars?

Anyone near the top of their field, whether it be a businessperson, a craftsman, an athlete, a politician, or a person with a close relationship with God, didn't get there by accident. They learned. They disciplined themselves to work hard at what they do, and they got help and training from others.

When we want to improve our hunting skills, we read books and talk to experienced hunters. If we want to learn to arrange flowers, we take a class or ask our aunt for tips.

Why shouldn't we apply this concept to getting along with other people? I'm pretty sure all of us have someone in our life who is good at relationships whom we could learn from. Unlike a training course or seminar, we won't even have to pay them.

Getting along with people means more than eliminating annoying or just plain bad habits and actions. We can make a meaningful difference in our ability to relate well to others by intentionally replacing those bad habits with good ones.

Think of at least two people you know who are easy to get along with. What makes them that way? I sat down one day and thought about people who are especially easy for me and others to get along with. I jotted down the following list:

- *They don't make you feel pressured to be a certain way or conform to their way of thinking.*
- *They listen well.*
- *They exude a caring attitude (accommodate my needs or wishes).*
- *They are nonconfrontational.*
- *They are able to laugh at themselves.*
- *They aren't worried about their reputation.*
- *They don't lose their tempers easily.*
- *They don't complain a lot.*

Then I surveyed some friends and sorted through their thoughtful responses describing someone they knew who was easy to get along with. I sorted the character traits and attributes they listed into six categories. To reveal how people's minds went in similar directions, I did not delete redundancies.

1. People who are easy to get along with are caring, interested in others, and good listeners.

They care about other people, and are interested in others.

They are very interested in others, remembering things others are involved in and asking interested questions.

They ask to talk about what interests me.

They relate with compassion.

They care for people no matter who they are.

They really listen and don't jump in to interrupt.

They listen when you talk and are respectful of your input even though they may not always agree.

They listen well, especially before responding.

They don't take sides quickly.

2. People who are easy to get along with are humble and do not act superior.

They are willing to admit they don't know something even if it makes them look foolish or dumb.

They don't have the air of "know-it-all" or "all put together."

They aren't afraid to say they don't know something or to not talk about something if they have limited or no knowledge about it.

They are humble—they don't give you a feeling of their superiority.

They do not always talk about themselves and their abilities, and they readily acknowledge when other people can do things better.

They realize the world is bigger than themselves and their experience and ideas.

They do good deeds, even in secret.

3. People who are easy to get along with are genuine and honest.

They are honest about themselves.

They are uninhibited—at ease, comfortable with themselves and with you.

They are comfortable in their own skin.

They are straightforward—you don't have to guess where they are coming from.

They rebuke without being judgmental—they don't avoid sharpening iron, but not in a belittling way; they don't ascribe motives, but speak to the behavior.

They are genuine.

They communicate about problems instead of bottling them up.

They take responsibility for things in their world and how they affect others.

4. People who are easy to get along with are thankful and focus on the positive.

They are unquenchable optimists.

They are sincere.

Their cups are half full.

They make positive comments instead of negative ones.

They tend to see the positive in people.

They are thankful about many things.

They don't talk negatively about others.

They are appreciative and express their appreciation.

They smile more than pout.

5. People who are easy to get along with are trustworthy and make others feel safe.

They are trustworthy; they won't tell everything they know or have heard to others.

Even when we have serious disagreements, they still like me.

They allow me to have a different opinion.

They forget disagreements easily.

They are not afraid to disagree, but not in a superior or "put-down" way.

They don't feel people have to be in a certain mold to be okay.

They are safe to share with—they are not shocked at my struggles.

They are respectful of all people.

They are very confidential.

When they need to give correction or encouragement they are not harsh.

They are dependable—I am never uncertain where I stand with them.

They are patient.

It is very, very hard to see any anger in them.

They are flexible, not pushy.

They know that everyone makes mistakes, and they accept them—both theirs and mine.

6. People who are easy to get along with are friendly and make others feel liked.

They are friendly, but not gushy or overly enthusiastic.

They make you feel like you are their friend—and they are that way to everyone.

They make me feel liked.

They don't fuss over serving me, but we can relax together.

I never feel intimidated in their presence.

They have a sense of humor—relaxing to be around, not stiff.

They are not ultra-busy nor do they measure the worth of a day (or a person) by how many tasks they completed.

Learn from these people. These are the qualities of people who are the best at relationships. The point of this chapter is not only to create a profile of someone who is easy to get along with, but to establish a goal we can aim for.

We probably already have several of these qualities, but to grow in our ability to get along, we can choose an area where we're weak and focus on it. Study other people as they relate and apply what you learn from them to this area in your own life. If you are purposeful about it, eventually it will become a habit or a character trait.

In any venture, if you aim at nothing, you are sure to hit it. Create purpose by making a picture of what you would like your relationships to look like one year from now. This will be a goal you see in the distance when you get tired of being nice to your coworkers.

You might write down a list like this:

I will communicate with my coworkers in a nonconfrontational way.
I will look for ways to keep peace in each of my relationships.
I will resolve conflicts upfront and not allow them to fester.
I will humbly allow others to have their way whenever I can.

TAKE IT TO WORK

1. Think of someone you know who is easy to get along with. What do you think makes them that way?
2. Identify one person in your workplace whom others seem to find easy to get along with. Observe his actions and attitudes to see what you can learn from them.
3. Which of the six characteristics in this chapter do you need to focus on? Think of a specific way you can practice each characteristic at work this week.

Chapter Nine

Become a Professional

When my wife and I went to a furniture chain store to purchase a chair, we came away planning to never go back. We almost regretted our decision to purchase from that store. What gave us this negative impression?

First, after we settled on which item to purchase, I had to give my name and address to two different people. Second, the salesman seemed to have written down the wrong product number or he had too many numbers on his paper and he couldn't find the right one. He trotted back out on the floor to jot down the number again while we waited patiently at the checkout desk.

Topping it off, the furniture store didn't have the item in stock, and they weren't sure when it would be available. They promised to call when it came in. A month later, I still hadn't heard from them.

Compare this to a shoe repair shop I stepped into for the first time not long after my furniture store experience. Not a computer was in sight, only racks and stacks of shoes and leather goods and several machines behind a counter.

The proprietor greeted me promptly and ran an experienced hand over the boots I had brought in. Without delay she told me what she would do to my boots, how much it would cost, and when I could pick them up again. She answered my questions, gave me a ticket on which to write my name and phone number, and I was out the door.

In spite of the old-timey atmosphere and lack of modern technology, I felt the cobbler was more of a professional than the furniture store employees. Not only did she treat me with respect, she knew her trade and how to best serve me.

Professionalism and getting along. Different people have different ideas of what "being professional" means, but we probably all agree that we'd like to be professional in our work. What does professionalism have to do with getting along with people?

Astronauts onboard the International Space Station must live and work together for months at a time. Getting along well with other people is crucial—an astronaut can't just leave if he can't stand a colleague.

The Code of Conduct for the International Space Station crew says, "ISS crewmembers' conduct shall be such as to maintain a harmonious and cohesive relationship among the ISS crewmembers and an appropriate level of mutual confidence and respect through an interactive, participative, and relationship-oriented approach which duly takes into account the international and multicultural nature of the crew and mission."[3]

Being professional isn't a cure-all for getting along with people at work, but it will help tremendously. When you act in a respectful, professional way, those you encounter in your work are more likely to respect you. Professional behavior doesn't cancel out personality differences, but it smooths out some of the bumps that cause problems in relationships on the job.

What makes a person professional? We sometimes think of a professional as someone who is highly educated and highly paid, such as a banker, lawyer, teacher, or engineer. However, anyone in any profession can act professionally even without years of education, decades of experience, or a high salary.

When I was a teenager someone told me that a professional was anyone who got paid to do what they do. (I joked that I was a professional boxer since my job was to pack products into boxes for shipping.)

Jokes aside, when we say that someone "was professional," a certain connotation or standard of conduct comes to mind. There are other definitions and ways to think about professionalism, but in this chapter I want to lay out the qualities that I believe are characteristics of professionals.

1. To be professional, know your organization or company. Broadly, this means having a general awareness of the mission, goals, and leaders of the company, as well as its position within its industry. More specifically, learn the ins and outs of the place where you work. Learn the company culture, how the company works, and how things get done at the company.

As long as we don't become busybodies and think we need to know everything that is going on at work, this contributes to our effectiveness and allows us to better understand and navigate the situations and problems we're involved with in the organization.

2. To be professional, support the organization. I have heard workers disparage their company and their leaders. While they may have had a reason for concern, this type of complaining is not the right thing to do.

Using the example of the code of conduct for the space station again, astronauts are forbidden from actions "adversely affecting the confidence of the public" in their work.

Being professional includes supporting the company, specifically its mission, goals, and leaders. Tearing down any of these things isn't just bad for the company, it's bad for us. It works against us by decreasing our effectiveness and dampening our enthusiasm. At the same time it's just plain discouraging to those around us.

3. To be professional, treat everyone the same. We wouldn't think of chewing out a customer, so let's not do that to our coworkers either. Treating everyone the same also means we don't allow ourselves to become part of a clique at work. Instead, we remain friendly and courteous to customers, coworkers, and superiors whether we agree with them or not.

What about showing the same level of respect to different levels of management? I know it's a lot easier to be respectful to the boss's boss when he comes around than it is to consistently be respectful to our "everyday" boss. It can be a challenge to be respectful of our direct supervisor because we know his weaknesses better, and his position isn't as high. Acting professionally means we respect authority, regardless of whether we feel our boss deserves it or not.

4. To be professional, do your best—without complaining. Being professional involves doing good work on each of the following type of jobs:

- Jobs we don't enjoy.
- Boring, easy tasks.
- Tough assignments.

Talking about our feelings with coworkers is one thing, but falling into the trap of being a negative person who habitually complains at work is another. Negativity is a breeding ground for trouble, and it's not professional.

5. To be professional, keep on learning. Even if you already know how to do your job well, determine to learn more. Learn more about your specific job, your company, and your industry. Even when we are on the lowest rung of the ladder at work, we can learn a lot by keeping our eyes and ears open.

If we ever reach the point of thinking we know all we need to know, we open ourselves up to incompetence, pride, and intellectual laziness.

6. To be professional, welcome both positive and negative feedback. Frank Clark said, "We find comfort among those who agree with us, and growth among those who don't." Learning from feedback and criticism is a good way to keep learning and growing. A professional doesn't fly off the handle when criticized, but tries to glean something useful from it even if he doesn't agree completely with it.

Both positive and negative feedback help us see things about our work and ourselves that we hadn't seen before. It helps us see the difference between what we think we are doing and what others see us doing—the difference between how we see ourselves and how others see us.

If we are perceptive, feedback tells us something about the other person. Is the boss a "detail person" or a "big picture" kind of person? What kind of actions and attitudes does he like to see? Feedback helps us find out, and we can then serve and relate to the boss (or coworker) better. In addition, it clarifies for us what the other person expects of us.

Have you ever asked your boss or your coworkers for feedback? The thought of inviting feedback can be intimidating and scary. *What if they say something I don't want to hear?* When we feel like we don't have a good sense of how we are doing, inviting feedback has several advantages. It makes us more approachable, strengthens the relationship, and opens our eyes to ourselves.

7. To be professional, be honest. Honesty and integrity should be priorities for us. We should be honest about:
- Our mistakes.
- Our product or service.
- Our weaknesses.
- Our time and expenses.

Be honest with your boss, your customers, your friends, and yes, even the coworkers you find hard to like. This doesn't mean we tell people everything on our minds, but when we make a mistake or miscalculation, we "fess up," not cover up. This builds trust, and doesn't give opportunity for others to accuse us of being too proud to admit mistakes.

We should try hard to keep our commitments at work, and let others know in advance if unforeseen situations will prevent us from doing so.

8. To be professional, communicate well. Communication is like lubricating oil that keeps a workplace healthy, productive, and efficient. Imagine an engine with no oil. Without communication, work slows down, mistakes happen, and frustration grows.

Communicate with everyone—your superiors, your peers, your subordinates. Communicate plans, expectations, instructions, context, and feedback. As a professional, learn to develop a good feel for answers to the following questions:
- What should I communicate in this situation?
- To whom should I communicate it?
- How much should I communicate?
- How should I communicate it?
- When should I communicate it?

9. To be professional, use systems for consistency and competence. Successful businesses use systems to accomplish large amounts of quality, consistent work. Our workplaces are full of systems, many of which we probably don't even notice.

To make yourself a better servant to your boss and your coworkers, adopt the concept of systems for your own workflow and procedures at work. This will make you more reliable and dependable and will help to increase others' confidence in you.

For example, have a filing system for emails or notes that you want to refer to later. Find the best way to do your everyday tasks and then follow that pattern daily. Have a place for tools and keep them in their place.

Acting like a professional requires more of us than just holding a job and collecting a paycheck. If we can go about our work quickly and competently, we have a good foundation for becoming a professional in our workplace. We will also find that professionalism will help us get along better with others. No one will be able to complain that we are not doing our work well.

John Oxenham's poem "Your Place" reminds us to be faithful in our work—for God's sake—no matter what our assignment.

> Is your place a small place?
> Tend it with care!
> He set you there.
>
> Is your place a large place?
> Guard it with care!
> He set you there.
>
> Whate'er your place, it is
> Not yours alone, but His
> That set you there.

TAKE IT TO WORK

1. Evaluate your actions and attitudes at work. Would an observer think of you as a professional? In which areas do you need to grow?
2. Identify someone at work whom you consider a professional. Think of one positive action or attitude you can change to become more like that person.
3. Select one characteristic of professionalism to work on this week. Think of one specific way you will begin to practice it.

Chapter Ten

Put Humility to Work for You

Are you a good driver? On a scale of 1 to 10, how would you rate your driving skills? Let me guess . . . a 7?

If you rated yourself above average (6-10), you have plenty of company. Studies demonstrate that people consistently tend to overestimate their own skill and abilities. For example, in one survey of driving skill, 93% of American participants rated themselves to be in the top 50% of drivers in the study! In another study, 80% of drivers considered themselves above average.[4] Apparently we have trouble coming to grips with the fact that our skills or intelligence might be below average.

The value of humility. David Dunning and Justin Kruger wrote a paper in 1999 titled, "Unskilled and Unaware of It: How Difficulties in Recognizing One's Own Incompetence Lead to Inflated Self-Assessments." They concluded that incompetent people often don't know they are incompetent, and that they overestimate their abilities.[5]

In his book *The Personal MBA,* Josh Kaufman calls this "excessive self-regard tendency."[6] Another name for it is simply *pride*. In the Bible, Proverbs says, "Let another man praise thee, and not thine own mouth; a stranger, and not thine own lips" (Proverbs 27:2).

What does this have to do with getting along with our coworkers? Thinking too highly of oneself usually stems from a proud heart, and pride poisons relationships. Proverbs says, "By pride comes nothing but strife, but with the well-advised is wisdom," and, "He who is of a proud heart stirs up strife" (Proverbs 13:10 and 28:25).

People who have excessively high regard for themselves have trouble getting along well with others. They consider themselves better than their coworkers. They want recognition and praise. They hand out lots of advice, but resist receiving any. They are slow to admit mistakes. They push others down, making themselves believe that they are lifting themselves up.

Do you work with anyone like this? Or do you think you might be one of these people with an "excessive self-regard tendency"? If so, you know from firsthand experience that none of these behaviors are good for relationships.

In his Gospel, Mark tells how James and John asked Jesus for seats of honor in His kingdom (see Mark 10:35-45). Not only did they seem to think they deserved to be treated better than the other disciples, but they vastly overestimated their abilities. Their request caused conflict with their coworkers, the other disciples.

A good way to help our relationships at work is to highly value the virtue of humility. In relationships, humility works in our favor. Making humility a priority and putting it to work for us frees us to be more productive—and easier to get along with.

Humility frees us to *do* our best rather than maintaining a front of *being* the best. We don't want to carry around the attitude of the politician who supposedly said, "I haven't been wrong since 1961, when I thought I made a mistake." Humility allows us to freely admit our weaknesses.

Being humble doesn't mean that we don't care about our work. It doesn't mean we can't put energy into excellence. A humble person can pursue excellence without being proud.

What is different about a humble person is that he is genuine about both his efforts and his flaws. He doesn't have to act like the best because he knows he isn't the best. He hasn't forgotten his humanity nor his ability to fail.

For example, one day Simon realized that he was no longer able to manage his workload. He had allowed himself to take on too many assignments, and he wasn't able to give them the time and energy they deserved.

Simon went to his boss and said, "I've overcommitted. It's my fault. I'm sorry. I don't have the capacity or capability to keep up. What can we do about it?" Even if you have never done this exercise yourself, you can imagine that it isn't ego-boosting!

When we live humbly, we no longer have to try to be perfect. We understand that we don't have to be better or appear better than others. Our goal is simply to be the best that we can be, regardless of how that compares to others. We acknowledge and use our strengths, but we don't try to hide our weaknesses.

We sometimes dislike others because they are better than us. Changing our focus from the proud focus of *being* the best to the humble focus of *doing* our best means it will no longer matter to us whether the other person is better than us or not. We no longer use them as a yardstick to measure ourselves. We can even be happy instead of jealous about their successes.

Humility frees us to learn from criticism rather than being defensive. I don't like criticism. Let me clarify, I don't like to *receive* criticism. On the other hand, when I am speaking critically of someone else, criticism doesn't bother me at all.

Criticism hurts, but it can help us see a side of ourselves that we have missed. Norman Vincent Peale said, "The trouble with most of us is that we would rather be ruined by praise than saved by criticism."

One wrong response to criticism is lashing out and attacking the other person. It is neither humble nor helpful to accuse the other person in order to excuse ourselves.

Another instinctive reaction is to become defensive. We spout off the reasons for doing what we did. Everyone understands there are reasons for what we did. Of course there are; otherwise we wouldn't have done it! But we don't always have to voice those reasons. A better way is to humbly listen to the criticism and try to learn from it. You may even want to try thanking them for their correction or criticism.

A humble person doesn't take criticism personally; he takes it professionally. Taking criticism humbly is taking it with a good attitude and looking for a lesson to learn. Even if the criticism feels unjustified, there is likely a grain of truth in it.

Humility frees us to learn from our mistakes rather than making excuses or ignoring other evidence. We miss many opportunities to learn just because we aren't ready or willing. An old proverb says, "When the pupil is ready, the teacher will appear."

The Bible says, "A reproof entereth more into a wise man than an hundred stripes into a fool" (Proverbs 17:10). A proud attitude can keep us from learning and growing.

We also tend to filter out information or evidence that goes against our decisions or ways of thinking. This habit, sometimes called confirmation bias, keeps us from learning new lessons. For example, if we like coffee, an article that claims coffee is good for us might inspire us to pass that information on to our friends, but we might not bother to read past the headline of a research article that indicates coffee or caffeine has a negative effect.

Another example: I can find myself replaying compliments in my mind for hours, but I shrug off the occasional rebuke or criticism that comes my way as not applying to me.

Why wouldn't I pay equal attention to both kinds of comments? Because the second kind goes against my preconceived opinion of the kind of person I am and the kind of work I do! I would probably learn more if I would turn that around and actually pay attention—humbly, not resentfully—to the negative comments.

Our tendency of filtering out or misinterpreting information that doesn't fit with our view of ourselves is likely one reason the people in the studies mentioned earlier rated their driving ability so highly.

Humility frees us to be a giver rather than a taker. Proud, selfish people try to pull others into an orbit around them like the planets orbit the sun. From their flawed perspective, they are the center of their universe and they want to be the center of ours too.

I find it too easy to think, "What can I get from my coworkers?" or "What can my coworkers do for me?" I should be asking, "What can I do for my coworkers?" and "How can I make a positive impact on my coworkers?"

The first attitude is a greedy, grabbing attitude; the second is a humble, giving attitude. Rather than forcing others to orbit around us, we can acknowledge their help and the contributions they have made to us. If we're willing to stop and think about it, we'll probably realize that all of our coworkers have blessed us or helped us in some way.

Asking questions like these can help us evaluate whether we are givers or takers at work:

- Do I freely offer to help others or do I expect something in return?
- Do I complain when others interfere with my work or do I willingly take time for their questions or problems?
- Do I talk a lot about my problems or do I listen to others? How often?
- Am I dependent or dependable?
- Do I need to feel in charge or am I happy to be a follower and servant?
- Do I avoid opportunities to help others or do I cheerfully accept them?
- Do I undermine and hold back others or do I support and encourage them?
- Do I feel secret satisfaction when others fail or am I pleased when they succeed?
- Do I need a lot of affirmation or do I work well even without feedback?

Humility frees us to learn from others rather than putting them down. One of George Washington's "Rules of Civility" is, "Undertake not to teach your equal in the art he himself professes; it savors of arrogancy." Washington realized that it's easier to dispense advice than it is to ask for it. Asking for help and learning from other people is an act of humility.

If we use the yardsticks of skill, income, or popularity to measure ourselves against our coworkers, we will have the never-ending chore of putting our coworkers down to make ourselves feel more secure.

The Pharisees of Jesus' day had this problem. Jesus was a newcomer.

The Pharisees felt threatened by His teaching and by His popularity. Because they loved the praise of people more than the praise of God, they felt they had to eliminate Jesus. Part of their reasoning was to protect their positions (see John 5:41-44 and John 11:47-53).

Sometimes it is hard for me to admit that I really don't know the best way to do something. If I'm humble, I'll admit my struggle to a coworker and ask him to show me how to do the task or improve my procedure. This can be especially difficult if it involves a newcomer at work. As the old pro, I might feel I should know more than the new person. Instead, I should recognize that fresh people in a workplace often have fresh ideas.

In reality, we owe everything we have and everything we are to others. Willingly learning from others is the only way we will ever learn anything, so we should accept and practice it at work.

Putting others down causes conflict and doesn't push us any higher. As the saying goes, "Blowing out someone else's candle doesn't make your own shine brighter." Living humbly—putting humility to work—allows us to encourage others, collaborate with them, and especially, to learn from them.

Benjamin Franklin wrote four tongue-in-cheek rules for making yourself "a disagreeable companion." The first one was to monopolize conversations and talk about how smart and successful you have been. "If possible engross the whole Discourse; and when other Matter fails, talk much of your-self, your Education, your Knowledge, your Circumstances, your Successes in Business, your Victories in Disputes, your own wise Sayings and Observations on particular Occasions."[7]

Franklin goes on to make the observation that by acting in this proud way, you will be able to please many people at one time—wherever you are *not*, people will be pleased that you are not there. (See appendix for all four of Franklin's rules.)

A humility check. As you probably know from experience, humility is remarkably freeing. Humble people are no longer chained to themselves. Humility increases our ability to work with others and makes it more enjoyable for them and us.

Most importantly, humility allows us to be on God's side rather than on the opposing side, because "God resisteth the proud, but giveth grace unto the humble" (James 4:6). And the opposing side never wins.

One way to check on our humility is to check how often we use these four humble phrases:
- "I am sorry."
- "I was wrong."
- "I need help."
- "I don't know."

If we can hardly bring ourselves to make statements like this, we likely aren't experiencing the blessing and the power of humility.

TAKE IT TO WORK

1. Choose a recent workday and evaluate your actions. Did they reveal humility, pride, or some of both? How were your relationships affected by your humility, or lack of it?
2. Analyze your relationship with a person you dislike. How does pride contribute to the tension?
3. Recall a rebuke you have received. Did you filter it out or seriously consider it to see if it was true? What will you do the next time you receive a rebuke or criticism?

Chapter Eleven

Practice Not Getting Offended

I remember a preacher saying, "I have decided to try to never get offended." It was such an outstanding statement that I never forgot it.

This preacher recognized that "getting offended" is a choice we make. When others do something against us, we can choose our response. People will offend us, but we don't have to get offended. Getting offended isn't automatic.

Let's think about the practice of getting offended and how we might be able to practice not getting offended at work.

Opportunities abound to be offended. As long as we are around other people, we will never run out of something to be offended about. There are many reasons we could get offended:

- A friend says something we don't like.
- A younger coworker doesn't respect us.
- The boss promotes someone else.
- The team rejects our proposal.
- A coworker assumes something untrue about us.
- The whole department chuckles at our mistake.

This world is an imperfect place, and our coworkers are imperfect people; they will trip up at times. We will offend others, too. James 3:2 says, "For in many things we offend all. If any man offend [or stumble] not in word, the same is a perfect man."

Getting offended is a result of taking something too personally. Sometimes we have genuine reason to be offended, but other times we don't. Not being chosen or allowed to do something that we really wanted to do is disappointing, but it doesn't equate to being rejected as a person.

I remember applying for a job one time. I went out for lunch with a manager, but the next week he let me know he wasn't interested. Disappointed, I felt like retorting "Why?" and arguing with the decision. I really had no reason to be offended except that my pride was hurt. I should not have taken the decision personally.

Getting offended can be a result of unfounded assumptions. In the Bible, King Saul was offended by David, who was many years his junior. When David had success in battle, including killing Goliath of whom Saul was afraid, David gained recognition and praise from the people.

Saul became suspicious and jealous of David; so jealous that he wanted to kill David. His belief that David planned to overthrow him was completely unfounded. Saul allowed his offended feelings to balloon into bitterness and deep-seated malice that controlled his life.

When we take offense, it's often because we jump to conclusions about the other person's motives. We assume they intended to hurt us. This is often untrue. Our coworkers don't usually come to work in the morning with a secret plan to hurt our feelings. We can deal with offenses better if we realize that the offense was probably unintentional.

Getting offended can be a result of majoring on minors. Let's say a coworker makes a comment about your new sweater. You're not sure what she meant, and you spend all morning turning it over in your head. In the end, is it really worth wasting mental energy on? In the long run, how much does your coworker's opinion of your sweater matter?

In the book of Esther, Haman was a proud royal advisor who became infuriated because one man among the crowd at the palace gates would not bow down to him. His angry response was completely out of proportion, and it eventually led to his own downfall.

Majoring on the minors happens when we make a big issue out of something that really deserves to be overlooked. Proverbs 19:11 says, "The discretion of a man deferreth his anger; and it is his glory to pass over a transgression."

Many—perhaps even most—of the opportunities we have to be offended fall into this category. Deciding to overlook one-time actions or comments is exactly what we would like others to do for us. We should graciously do it for them.

Getting offended happens less when we know and understand our coworkers well. Think about your closest friends. How often do they offend you? Probably not very often. This illustrates how communication and strong relationships fend off offenses. We more easily understand our friends' true motives or what they really intended to communicate.

When you know and like someone fairly well, you aren't as tempted to be offended by what they do and say. Friends like this have your respect. Furthermore, you know without even asking that they didn't mean to hurt you, because you know their character and heart.

You might think that the less two people communicate, the less likely they are to misunderstand each other and the less chance they have of getting offended. However, the reverse is often true. The less two people communicate with each other at work, the more likely they are to misunderstand each other's actions and motives when frustrations or conflicts arise.

The saying that "imagination starts where communication stops" holds true at work. When we aren't communicating well with our coworkers, we can start imagining the worst about their motives.

Martin Luther King, Jr. said, "People fail to get along because they fear each other; they fear each other because they don't know each other; they don't know each other because they have not communicated with each other."

Offenses are opportunities to grow. When we respond in the right way, offenses are stepping-stones to growth in our personal and professional life. Responding in kind or holding a grudge are wrong responses. As someone has said, "Holding a grudge is like drinking poison and expecting the other person to die."

We can deal graciously with offenses by disciplining ourselves to:

- Give the benefit of the doubt.
- Remember that getting offended is a choice.
- Overlook the offense.
- Decide to not take it personally.
- Be willing to laugh at ourselves.
- Use it as a stepping-stone to growth.

Thomas à Kempis had some good advice: "Let not thy peace depend on the tongues of men, for whether they judge well or ill, thou art not on that account other than thyself."

TAKE IT TO WORK

1. Describe how you typically feel and respond when you "get offended." Does this response help the situation?
2. Identify a time you felt offended. Examine any assumptions you made about the other person. Are they fact or fiction? Ask someone who is not in the situation to help you look at it objectively.
3. List four ways you can respond graciously to an offense. Use them the next time you are tempted to get offended.

Part Two
Working with Others

Chapter Twelve

Apologize for Real

Ryan was having trouble getting along with Joe, who worked on the same crew. The position of excavator operator had just opened up, and Ryan badly wanted the job. To his deep disappointment, his boss gave the job to Joe. Joe got the fun, comfy job of sitting in the cab, while Ryan did hard, dirty work outside on the ground.

One day Ryan and Joe were assigned to work together laying concrete pipe in a deep ditch. Joe was operating the excavator, which had a chain attached to its arm. Ryan's job was to attach the chain to the concrete pipe. After the excavator lifted the heavy pipe and swung it over and down into the ditch, Ryan would unhook the chain.

In Ryan's own words, he "wasn't being very workable." Exasperated, Joe swiveled the arm of the excavator in such a way that the chain hit Ryan. Almost without thinking, Ryan reached down for a small rock and flung it at Joe—and his aim was good. *Thunk!*

Remember that sinking feeling we get when we realize we messed up—again? What are we supposed to do next? How can we fix the problem we created?

1. Own up. The first step in fixing the relationship is to take responsibility and simply admit we made a mistake. In Ryan's situation, Joe was partly at fault—he contributed to the frustration Ryan was feeling by swinging the chain at him. Yet Ryan was the one who threw the rock. He could not blame Joe for that.

Owning up to our mistakes takes a big dose of humility coupled with courage. We have to forget about trying to look good and resist the temptation to pretend that nothing happened. Or if something really did happen it certainly wasn't our fault.

Saving the relationship is more important than saving face. Making excuses for ourselves doesn't help us or the other person.

When we take responsibility to make things right with the coworker we have hurt, we send the message that the relationship—and the person—are valuable to us. When we get defensive or ignore the problem, we send the opposite message.

2. Apologize. One time I really upset a coworker. I didn't mean to, but I was clearly at fault. I'm not sure how it came up, but I jokingly said something like, "What kind of person would want to marry you?"

I knew the second it left my mouth that it was a mistake. I knew it even before my coworker turned and walked stiffly away. The first thing I did was kick myself. The second was to look for a chance to apologize. To help restore the relationship, I had no choice but to admit I was wrong and apologize.

A good, simple apology is, "I am sorry. I was wrong." These may be only six words, but they are six of the hardest words we will ever say. Too often we live in our own little bubble in which we are at the center of everything. However, the world does not revolve around us. "I was wrong" acknowledges that other people and their feelings are important too.

Eleanor Farjeon's intriguing little poem "The Quarrel" illustrates how admitting our mistakes and apologizing turns the relationship around and turns us from being in the wrong to being in the right.

> I quarreled with my brother,
> I don't know what about,
> One thing led to another

And somehow we fell out.
The start of it was slight,
The end of it was strong,
He said he was right,
I knew he was wrong!

We hated one another.
The afternoon turned black.
Then suddenly my brother
Thumped me on the back,
And said, "Oh, come on!
We can't go on all night—
I was in the wrong."
So he was in the right.

3. Be genuine. Eating humble pie isn't easy. Apologizing isn't easy. Human nature makes us want to justify our actions. Of course there was a reason for what we did; otherwise we wouldn't have done it! But that's not the point of any apology. Whether or not we intentionally offended or hurt the other person, the fact is that we *did*.

We have to be genuine when we apologize. This means we don't try to defend ourselves. Usually we shouldn't even try to explain ourselves, because this sounds defensive. When someone is hurting, or perhaps upset with us, in their minds there is not much difference between an explanation and an excuse. What sounds like an explanation to me will sound like an excuse to him.

Being genuinely sorry means we don't try to shift the blame. If we use words like "if" or "but," the person we've hurt will know we aren't genuine. The apology will mean nothing.

Have you heard "apologies" like these?

"I'm sorry I hurt you, but I didn't mean to."

"If what I did yesterday offended you, I apologize."

"Please forgive me for what I said, but you know I was having a stressful day."

4. Ask forgiveness. When we mess up, we can't force the offended party to forgive us, but we can make it easier for them to do so. Coworkers are less likely to forgive us if we don't ask for it. Plus, they usually want us to ask for it. They want us to admit we were wrong so they can tell we are genuinely sorry. If we don't, they may build a wall that keeps us at a safe distance.

To ask someone for forgiveness, add a few more words to the first six we looked at. "I am sorry. I was wrong. Will you forgive me?"

One friend told me that once when he asked a coworker for forgiveness, he got only the silent treatment. Because forgiveness can come hard, we may need to add, "I would like your forgiveness, but can understand that you might not be ready to forgive right now." This takes the pressure off the other person and gives them time to process it.

Even if our coworker doesn't feel like offering forgiveness, we will have done our part, and can walk away gracefully. Whether or not the hurtful words or actions were intentional, when we take responsibility, apologize, and ask forgiveness, we open a door that will allow restoration.

5. Show compassion and contrition. When rebuilding a relationship, two words to remember are *compassion* and *contrition*. We can make compassion part of our apology by empathizing with the other person, acknowledging their hurt, and doing what we can to heal the situation. We can show contrition by showing that we genuinely regret what happened and accept responsibility for it. We learned from the mistake and we won't do it again.

In the case of our rock-throwing friend, compassion and contrition touched Joe's heart. Ryan knew he had messed up. Ryan knew he had not acted the way Jesus would want him to. He was determined to heal the relationship he had broken.

Ryan decided to win Joe with kindness. Knowing Joe liked Pepsi, Ryan started bringing a can of Pepsi along back to the job site from the deli where he ate lunch. The first time, Joe refused to touch it. Over the next few days, Ryan persisted, and each day he bought another soft drink for Joe.

Eventually Joe acknowledged the peace offering and began accepting the drinks Ryan offered. Due to Ryan's determination to reach out, the relationship continued to heal, and the two men worked together well. In fact, when Ryan left for another job later, Joe begged him to stay.

That is the amazing power of an apology!

> **TAKE IT TO WORK**
>
> 1. Which do you value more: saving a relationship or saving face? Describe the effect of an apology on a relationship.
> 2. What are specific words and actions that prove the sincerity of your apology?
> 3. What should you do if the offended person doesn't accept your apology?

Chapter Thirteen

Improve Your Approachability

A few years ago a stray cat started hanging around our place. We put food out for her, and not surprisingly, she made herself at home. We named her Maggie.

It took several weeks for Maggie to warm up to us, but even after she let us get close enough to pet her, we noticed she was still very jumpy. When we walked by her, she would watch our feet like a hawk. Perhaps at her previous home she had been on the receiving end of some well-aimed kicks. Maggie had learned not to trust feet.

Unapproachability = isolation. Like Maggie, have you ever felt jumpy and unsafe around certain people? I have. On the flip side, probably a few people have felt unsafe being around me. Not that they feared I would kick them, but they feared being emotionally hurt by my words or actions.

Our coworkers will act just like Maggie if they don't trust our reactions. If we frequently hurt our coworkers, they will learn to stay away from us. If they never know when they will step on a land mine, they'll stay out of our territory. Flying off the handle and hitting the ceiling doesn't only hurt your head, it hurts your coworkers' hearts.

When our coworkers avoid us this way, we will become isolated from workplace camaraderie as they stop sharing their thoughts and experiences with us. People will be afraid to alert us when they notice something going wrong. Because they will become accustomed to avoiding us, they probably won't even congratulate us when we do something right.

What else happens if we become isolated?

- We are more likely to be left out of the loop on important conversations and decisions.
- We lose opportunities to contribute our point of view or expertise.
- We experience less fulfillment and more frustration at work.
- We develop a warped view of reality because we are no longer seeing the full picture.
- We are more likely to be cynical (and wrong) about others' motives and their work.

This is not the kind of environment we want to work in! How can we improve our approachability and keep this from happening to us?

Pay attention to how people approach you. We all want people to let us know (kindly) when we're doing something wrong or when there is an area in which we can improve. They won't give us this favor if we are not approachable. The best way to increase our approachability is to make others feel safe around us.

I liked jokes and ridiculous sayings when I was young. Somewhere I picked up this little ditty: "Tie a donkey to a tree / Pull its tail and think of me." I can only imagine what happens when you pull a donkey's tail, but I assume it is something painful and that the backside of a donkey must be approached with care.

We can find out how our coworkers approach us by paying attention. Are they nervous? Do they hesitate to ask us a question? Do they avoid bringing up issues because they are afraid of our reaction? If the answer is yes, then people don't feel safe around us.

Review your typical responses. Why would someone hesitate to approach me with a question at work? Perhaps they got hurt by someone like me before, or I may have hurt them in the past. Maybe I appear too busy to talk to them or they perceive me as uncaring. Perhaps I somehow make them uncomfortable.

To help think through why someone might hesitate to approach you, think about the times that you hesitate to approach someone else. What were the reasons? Did you perceive them as being unkind, sensitive, or defensive? We can check ourselves to see if any of those reasons might apply to our relationships with others.

I have found that I get into the habit of responding in certain ways to certain people. For example, with certain coworkers I subconsciously feel the need to justify my actions. Evaluating our responses to people throughout the week helps us be aware of the ways we might be diminishing our approachability.

Focus on building trust. Improving approachability is an exercise in building trust. So when someone comes up to me with a question, comment, or concern, I should think, "How can I respond in a way that will help this person trust me?"

This doesn't mean that we have to respond the way the person wants us to. For example, if our coworker makes a request, building trust and improving approachability doesn't mean that we have to always say, "Yes! Sure thing!"

We can give our coworkers a break by:
- Responding to new ideas with openness instead of scorn.
- Responding to questions with answers rather than exasperation.
- Responding to unsolicited advice with, "Thanks for that. I'll think about it," rather than telling them off.
- Responding to criticism (even unwarranted) with a pleasant attitude rather than lashing back.

As your coworkers find out that approaching you is not such an ordeal after all, they will learn that you are a safe person—someone who won't hurt them.

Be willing to be sharpened. "Iron sharpeneth iron; so a man sharpeneth the countenance of his friend" (Proverbs 27:17). Iron sharpens iron only when both sides are willing to be part of the process. This generally only happens when both sides are secure in their role and have a connection built on trust and respect.

I remember when one of my superiors was hesitant about something

I fully supported. When he voiced a doubt, I listened. Then I made my case. Through our shared history of working together, I had learned that it was safe to voice an opposing opinion. I knew that he valued my ideas even if I differed.

When we have a strong relationship with our coworkers, their pointed questions do not hurt us or the relationship. They are simply part of doing the best work in the best way possible. If others are afraid to challenge our ideas or ask questions, it means they don't feel safe around us.

Be less moody and more consistent. With some people you just don't know what to expect when you get to work. They are more fickle than the weather—one day they greet you with a smile but the next day with a snap and a snarl.

In general, people feel safe with predictability. They like to sit at the same desk in the same chair drinking the same brand of coffee they did yesterday. Likewise, they don't like when their coworkers are moody one day and irrationally exuberant the next.

Whether they have good or bad news, our coworkers shouldn't have to jab a barometer into our space to gauge our mood before they approach us. Our coworkers would appreciate the gift of consistency. They want to know what to expect when they walk into our office, and if we are predictably kind and polite, they will come to like and trust us.

Depending on how you think about it, having a coworker who is predictably unkind is in some ways preferable to having one who is sometimes sugary sweet and other times harsh and angry. If someone is predictably unpleasant, at least everyone knows what to expect and can prepare accordingly.

If I kindly compliment someone in the morning, then yell at them in the afternoon, that person will think twice about coming up to me about something. They may just decide not to talk to me about it at all.

Your coworkers will perceive you as a threat if you are unpredictable. Conversely, each day that you respond with the same pleasant demeanor and affability, you are training them to trust you as an approachable person.

TAKE IT TO WORK

1. Think of people you find easy to approach and identify reasons why they are easily approachable.
2. Observe how your coworkers approach you. Do they come warily or freely? How does your behavior (past or present) affect their approach?
3. List two ways improving your approachability will improve your effectiveness at work.

Chapter Fourteen

Say "Good Morning" to Your Coworkers

In some regions of the country, everyone waves at everyone else they meet on the road. Farmers in their pickups on the way to the farm or to the café, workers in their cars headed for the office—everyone has a nod and a wave, or at least a friendly finger wiggle, for each vehicle they meet on the road.

Does your workplace have a similar morning custom? Do workers have a friendly greeting for those they meet in the morning? Or do people mostly ignore each other or give only a grumpy-sounding grunt?

A friend told me that when she started a new job, in the morning her new coworkers would carefully avoid looking at her, preferring to remain in their own little shells. It made her feel unappreciated—as though she didn't count.

Whether you work in a factory, a job site outdoors, or an office setting, saying "good morning" is a good way to start the day. I once had a coworker whose goal was to say "good morning" to every person he met at work in the morning. He tried to initiate the greeting before they spoke to him.

I was once just the opposite. In school I had a teacher who I didn't really like. When she said "good morning" to me when I walked into the classroom each morning, I rarely responded.

At the time I didn't realize how rude my actions were. Though I'm not always consistent, I now make it a practice to try to say "good morning" to my coworkers. I also use the greeting in morning emails as a nice way to start the conversation.

Even if you aren't a "morning person" you can learn this good communication habit. It's quick, easy, and doesn't cost anything. If you dread communicating with others first thing in the morning, you will benefit from saying "good morning" because it helps ease your way into the morning.

Consider these reasons for saying "good morning" to people at work.

1. "Good morning" is polite, welcoming, and kind. Saying "good morning," just like saying "please" and "thank you," is a courteous thing to do. Common courtesies, though small things, make the world a nicer place. They are like a lubricant that can help keep people relating to each other smoothly.

Saying "good morning" is not only a greeting, it is also wishing our coworker well for the day. In that sense, saying "good morning" takes us out of our own little world and helps us pay attention to someone else. For at least a second it takes our thoughts off ourselves and how our own morning is going (or not going). Focus on the other person and genuinely wish him a good day.

2. "Good morning" acknowledges the other person's presence. The other person is obviously present, so we should go ahead and acknowledge that. A "good morning" goes at least a little way toward making others feel welcomed.

Ignoring a person is rude. Diving immediately into business with a command or question with no welcome or greeting could be considered rude too. People like to be noticed and are glad to know that you care they are there.

3. "Good morning" is an easy way to break the silence. If we don't speak to a coworker when they arrive, then sometimes we don't feel like speaking to them at all. It's like we've missed our best chance to get the day's communication off to a good start.

If the other person begins work for the day without speaking to us, the silence can go on and on. The longer it goes, the harder it can be to break. We share the same space and oxygen, so why not share words?

4. "Good morning" is an easy way to start a conversation. Conversations at work are important. Many of the things that make a workplace pleasant—camaraderie, friendships, a congenial atmosphere—revolve around conversations.

Saying "good morning" each morning is an easy way to get the day's conversations off to a pleasant start. It allows us to approach our coworker with what we have to say. Conversely, if our coworker has been hesitating to discuss something with us, or has been waiting for the right opportunity, a greeting gives him an opening.

5. "Good morning" provides a glimpse into the other person's day. Our coworkers will respond to our greeting either in a positive, negative, or neutral way. If they are harboring animosity toward us, their response might reveal their heart.

For example, they could respond like I responded to my teacher—by ignoring the greeting. Hopefully they will return the greeting cheerfully, but they could also respond with a negative comment like, "No, it's not."

If we are alert to our coworkers' responses, we can sense their mood. Hopefully we can then respond in a way that blesses them or meets their need at the moment.

Saying "good morning" to our coworkers doesn't automatically make us everyone's friend, yet it's a good practice to have. We can make it personal and genuine by saying it pleasantly and making eye contact. In small ways, it will make a positive difference in our relationships at work.

TAKE IT TO WORK

1. How do you feel if your coworker doesn't greet you in the morning? In what ways could a friendly greeting improve your relationships at work?
2. Observe someone at your workplace who offers a friendly greeting in the morning, and someone who doesn't. Does this relate to their attitude the rest of the day? How?
3. If you are hesitant to initiate a friendly greeting in the morning, can you identify the reason why?

Chapter Fifteen

Communicate Courtesy and Encouragement

Years ago I had a supervisor who took special care to wish me well on my birthday. I remember him saying he was glad I worked in his department and that he appreciated my work. Because of this, I enjoyed working for him, and he stands out in my memory even today.

I still have a note that another boss wrote on one of my first paycheck stubs. It reads,

"Caleb, it's good to have you on the team. Keep up the good work."

A year later, he wrote another one:

"Caleb, it's been good working with you this past year. May the Lord direct you in your position."

The more time we spend with someone, the more we influence them. Each day at work we have countless opportunities to encourage and to bless our coworkers by what we say. Are we taking these opportunities or wasting them with cynical, unkind, or discouraging comments?

Simple courtesies count. My mom used to say, "What's the magic word?" when I neglected to preface a request with the word "please." Be grateful if your mom was like mine, because it is likely more important that you say "please" and "thank you" in your work today than it was when you were growing up.

Common courtesies make a small but noticeable difference any time human beings share the same space day after day. Imagine a world where no one told you, "Thanks." What if no one ever said, "Excuse me," when accidentally getting in your way?

In addition to using "Please," "Thank you," and "Excuse me" as much as possible, we can learn polite ways of saying words like "No," "Later," and "I have a better way," that carry a negative message. Speaking courteously to everyone at work—customers, peers, superiors, or subordinates—makes them feel respected and not like just a machine or animal.

There are other ways to express courtesy in the way we talk to our coworkers. Instead of talking in a tone that sounds belittling or demanding, the same information or question can be reworded and voiced more respectfully.

Aristotle said, "It is not enough to know what we ought to say; we must also say it as we ought." In addition to *tone*, we may need to adjust the *timing* and the *temperature* of the comment.

For example, if a machine is broken down and slowing production, you might ask in frustration, "How long are we to limp along like this?" Your boss might appreciate a more respectful tone at a less stressful moment: "Do you think we will be limping along like this for a while?"

Government diplomats are usually very careful to be courteous in their communications with other countries. President Abraham Lincoln's Secretary of State once wrote a sharp message to Great Britain, saying that Lincoln was "surprised and grieved" and that certain actions by Great Britain would not "be borne" or allowed by the United States.

When Lincoln reviewed the letter before it was sent, he made some changes to soften its tone. Instead of saying that he was "surprised and grieved," Lincoln changed it to read that the "President regrets" their actions. Instead of saying that the United States would not bear certain actions, he revised it to say the actions wouldn't "pass unnoticed."[8]

Encouragement gives courage. According to one of my coworkers, I used to respond with, "You are so stupid," to some of her ideas. Frankly,

I don't remember this, but I believe her. It sounds exactly like something I would do! I don't think I meant it seriously, but even so, it wasn't encouraging, and my coworker didn't like it.

Encouraging words make a huge difference to people. They make a difference for those who receive them, those who say them, and those who overhear them.

In *Winning with People,* John Maxwell gives the THINK acronym for evaluating our words. Sarcastic or cynical remarks won't make it through this filter.

> T - Is it true?
> H - Is it helpful?
> I - Is it inspiring?
> N - Is it necessary?
> K - Is it kind?[9]

We can think of encouragement as giving courage. A coworker you have encouraged is empowered to move ahead with courage, with confidence, with a laugh, with an extra spring in his step. Our workplace and the world both need more encouragers, and you can be one of them.

Here are some ideas of simple, encouraging things to say.

- I'm glad you're helping us with this.
- Good idea!
- That turned out nice. Can you show me how you did it?
- You are good at this.
- Do you mind if I give you a hand?
- I hope this project goes well for you.

Blaise Pascal wrote, "Cold words freeze people, and hot words scorch them, and bitter words make them bitter, and wrathful words make them wrathful. Kind words also produce their own image on men's souls; and a beautiful image it is. They smooth, and quiet, and comfort the hearer."

Sometimes it is helpful to examine the results, or the fruit, of our words. Do our words bear good fruit, helping others take courage, or do our comments depress and dismay them?

As important as words are, not all encouragement comes in the form of words. Sometimes all it takes to give someone a boost is silence and a listening ear. For example, have you ever sat down and just listened as a coworker talked about something that was bothering him? Talking things over with a trusted friend helps us feel better.

Who needs encouragement? We all do. No matter how confident or enthusiastic a boss or coworker may seem, occasionally he or she too will have a down day and need an encouraging word. If you're observant and caring, you can be the one to give it.

Optimism is important. A good exercise is to think back over your day at work. Review in your mind the day's conversations. What topics did you discuss? Did you make mostly negative or mostly positive comments?

Negative thoughts include pessimistic or cynical comments. A pessimist or cynic sees only the worst side of every situation. A pessimist thinks that if things appear to be going better, you must have overlooked something. A cynic chooses to cast doubts and believe the worst about everything.

There are a multitude of cynical jokes about work and coworkers. Here is a cynical comment about committees: "A committee of three gets things done, if two don't show up." And here is another one: "Teamwork is essential. It allows you to blame someone else."

In contrast, the Bible speaks positively about both work and teamwork: "If any would not work, neither should he eat" (2 Thessalonians 3:10). "For by wise counsel thou shalt make thy war: and in multitude of counsellors there is safety" (Proverbs 24:6).

It's true that most situations, products, and people have flaws or issues that could be improved. The thing about cynics is that their own accusations unwittingly illustrate the unsavory side of human nature they gleefully highlight in others.

By focusing on the negative or the potential negative, pessimists and cynics ignore the good or positive things they could see if they wanted to. Worse, they drag others down into the dumps with them.

In the second stanza of his poem "The House by the Side of the Road," Sam Walter Foss resolves to be a friend rather than a scorner or cynic.

Let me live in a house by the side of the road
Where the race of men go by—
The men who are good and the men who are bad,
As good and as bad as I.
I would not sit in the scorner's seat
Nor hurl the cynic's ban—
Let me live in a house by the side of the road
And be a friend to man.

Here are a few ideas for being a friend who shows or promotes optimism:
- Challenge unsubstantiated pessimistic remarks.
- Don't let the minority pessimist rule.
- Highlight things that went right.
- Keep your facial expression pleasant and your body language relaxed.
- Ward off that feeling of being overwhelmed by breaking projects down into more simple, doable pieces.
- Pass up opportunities to criticize everything that goes wrong.
- Present the big picture to those who are only looking at the small picture.

In addition to brightening the picture, choosing to emphasize what is good and right encourages more good and right behavior. This is illustrated by a neat twist on an old saying: "The grass is greener where you water it."

Every workplace can benefit from a few more people who believe the light at the end of the tunnel is indeed the end of the tunnel, not an oncoming train. Through our encouraging words, people can walk away from us better off than when they came.

TAKE IT TO WORK

1. Identify the coworkers you spend the most time with. Do you tend to encourage or discourage them? Name a specific way you can encourage them this week.
2. Review your daily behavior at work. In what areas or circumstances should you be more courteous?
3. When problems arise can you see the opportunity hidden in the problem or do you see only the problem?

Chapter Sixteen

Compliment Your Coworkers

Mark Twain said, "I can live for two months on a good compliment." I can identify with that sentiment. Compliments make me feel better about myself and my work.

Compliments are a good way to boost our relationships at work. If we can develop the habit of giving compliments, we will be much better at getting along with people. It's an encouraging boost for them—and benefits us too. One genuine compliment can motivate a person more than one hundred scoldings.

Compliments don't have to be verbal. One morning I arrived at work and was surprised to find a picture of a large gold medal hanging in my office. The medal had my name on it, and read, "Quality Writer." The source was anonymous, but I soon identified and thanked the coworker it came from. I appreciated the sentiment of course, and even more so because of the time he had taken to design, print out, and cut out the medal.

In *The Three Signs of a Miserable Job*, Patrick Lencioni says that we are miserable at work when we feel unnoticed and irrelevant, and when we can't see or measure our progress. Giving compliments to our coworkers for what they are doing is a small way we can make them feel noticed and appreciated. A compliment will get their attention. All of our coworkers, even if they seem self-confident or indifferent, will notice—and remember—what we say.[10]

Compliments are for everyone. No doubt you can think of someone at work who does not deserve a compliment. His attitude is unpleasant and you don't see anything good about him at all. Take up the challenge of finding something about that person to praise.

We have to admit that even people we don't like still have positive attributes. Is he a steady worker? Loyal to another coworker in the office? Neat and organized? Good with customers? Good with words? Efficient? Just like the saying that every cloud has a silver lining, every coworker has something that we can compliment.

Complimenting people helps us to think more positively about them. Have you ever noticed that it is hard to act nice to someone you despise? Getting rid of our negative thoughts about someone is critical to getting rid of negative actions like snide remarks, cold shoulders, and defensiveness that are bad for relationships.

Complimenting others helps keep us from complaining about them. Conjuring up a genuine compliment (if that is what it takes) helps push out some of the ugly thoughts we have about that coworker. Complimenting others will help them think more positively about us too. We tend to think positively about people who say good things about what we do.

Complimenting people helps us see their strengths. If we find it difficult to like someone, their faults are much more glaring than their talents. That is often our problem rather than theirs, because our perspective is skewed. We become like a piece of Velcro, grabbing onto everything we think they are doing wrong, no matter how small.

Training ourselves to see people's strengths takes discipline. As we notice what our coworkers are good at—even if we may feel they are good at very little—we will find it easier to appreciate them.

One schoolteacher took extra time several times a year to write a compliment to each student. She would place it in their math books where they would be sure to notice it the next day. This was as much for her sake as for the students'. These notes helped her remember her students' good points instead of only pushing them for improvements.

The teacher told me, "My notes would not have worked so well if I had 'clarified' them with reminders about the areas I wanted them to improve in. They already knew that stuff. This was my time to say, 'I notice something you do really well!' and leave it at that."

Compliments are motivational. A compliment lets a person know that someone is noticing their work and cares about how they do their work. Compliments make our coworkers try harder to be a better person or to do a better job.

One of my coworkers told me, "Compliments from people who are the kind of people I like to receive compliments from are humbling (as in, I need to live up to this) and they can make me want to be a better person (as in I WANT to live up to that)."

Compliments are easy to give. We may not think of ourselves as the type of people who hand out a lot of compliments, yet we probably do it all the time—with our good friends. Comments like "Hey, that looks good!" and "I wish I could do that as well as you can" come more easily when we are addressing someone we like a lot.

It may not come naturally at first, especially if you have a habit of putting people down rather than building them up, but it only takes a few seconds and a few words to compliment someone.

Compliments should not include flattery. Our sincere compliments will make our coworkers feel noticed, appreciated, and valued. In contrast, a compliment that a coworker perceives as flattery will mean nothing to him. In fact, it will likely make the relationship worse. Compliments need to be true.

Proverbs 29:5 says, "A man that flattereth his neighbour spreadeth a net for his feet." If we gush to a coworker about something he is not sure is true about himself, he will become uncertain rather than more confident. He may wonder if we are trying to get something from him in return. Meaningful compliments have depth and sincerity.

Sarcastic compliments aren't compliments. When it comes to relationships that are already tense, sarcasm is deadly. A compliment laced with sarcasm hurts, and it kills opportunities for relationships to improve. Saying, "Great! It was so helpful that you arrived on time this morning," when someone walks in thirty minutes behind schedule doesn't help the situation at all.

Instead of inspiring the latecomer to do better, it is more likely to turn him against you. Try a gentle rebuke instead: "I was disappointed that we are getting a late start." If the person shows up on time the next day, compliment and thank him.

Compliments are a good way to apply the Golden Rule. If we like to receive them, we should give them too.

TAKE IT TO WORK

1. How do you feel toward people who genuinely compliment you?
2. Think of two coworkers you struggle to get along with. Identify one thing you appreciate about each person and compliment them when you get a chance.
3. Evaluate the compliments you give to your coworkers. Why do you give compliments? Are you trying to get something from them? Encourage them to improve? Flatter them? Resolve to give only sincere compliments, and to do it as often as appropriate.

Chapter Seventeen

Put Yourself in Others' Shoes

Steve was on his way home from work in Washington D.C. and Interstate 66 was at a crawl like usual, all lanes packed with vehicles inching along. Steve darted into another lane of traffic, cutting off a car behind him.

When that car passed him a bit later, the driver made a rude gesture. Steve started to stew. He hadn't done anything wrong—he was just driving like you have to drive in bumper-to-bumper traffic.

Later the traffic came to a standstill. Lights from emergency vehicles told Steve there was an accident ahead. Along with everyone else, he sat waiting, the car with the finger-waving couple directly ahead. The driver, an older gentleman, got out and walked back toward Steve.

Apprehensive, Steve rolled down his window. What now? "I had nothing against you," Steve said hastily. "I just needed to get into this lane."

But the driver had come to apologize. "I'm sorry," he said. "We should not have been upset at you. I know you didn't mean anything by it. Our daughter was killed in a car accident on I-395 earlier this week. We are on the way home from her funeral."

Suddenly the whole picture changed. Rather than stewing at the couple's reaction to the way he cut in front of them, Steve now had the deepest empathy for them. He now understood their actions. "I'm so sorry," he said.

The Golden Rule says to treat others the way you want to be treated. Two ways we can practice the Golden Rule are to empathize with others and to give them a second chance when they mess up.

What is empathy? Empathy is the ability to understand and share another person's emotions or feelings. When we empathize, we share their feelings and experiences as much as we can.

We find it easy to empathize with babies and young children. When my daughter, who can sit up but not crawl, tips over backward and thumps her head on the floor, I can almost feel her pain. I pick her up, hug her close, and speak soothing words.

To some people, work is a place to be tough and simply get the job done. They aren't used to giving or receiving emotional support. Even this type of coworker needs empathy. Perhaps someone in their family dies, or some other stressful situation comes up. How can we show empathy at work?

Show that you care. If you have a dog, has he or she ever approached you when you were sad or upset and nuzzled your hand? Your dog responded to your emotional state and showed that she cared about you.

Theodore Roosevelt said, "People don't care how much you know until they know how much you care." Whether or not our coworkers like us as a person doesn't depend on our efficiency, productivity, or creativity. We may have brilliantly creative ideas, but if we are self-centered and focused only on ourselves and our problems, our coworkers still won't like us.

When a coworker is hurting or distressed, we can show that we care through something we say, something we do, or a gift we give. We might give them a card or take up a donation if they are experiencing a need.

When the father of one of my coworkers died, we bought a special flower for her. The flower will bloom each year, reminding her of her father, and also reminding her that her coworkers care about her. Another way to show that we care is to take up the slack without complaining if a coworker needs some time off work.

Showing that we care about our coworkers goes a long way toward helping them like us. This is easy to understand, because we like the people who care about us.

This poem by Emily Dickinson reminds us how important it is to care for those around us.

> If I can stop one heart from breaking,
> I shall not live in vain;
> If I can ease one life the aching,
> Or cool one pain,
> Or help one fainting robin
> Unto his nest again,
> I shall not live in vain.

Put yourself in others' shoes. An old proverb encourages us to never criticize someone until we have walked a mile in his moccasins. We can't do this perfectly, but we can try to put ourselves in someone else's shoes.

This requires us to imagine how another person might be feeling about the situation he finds himself in. In addition to imagining, we can remember how we may have felt in a similar situation in the past. We can use reverse perspective and ask, *How would I feel if I was that person?*

When we treat others the way we want to be treated, we will speak healing words instead of hurting words. If my coworker just realized he made a thousand-dollar mistake, I shouldn't say, "That was stupid!" (even if it was).

Instead, I should pause and try to formulate a sympathetic reply such as, "I'm sorry it had to happen to you. It will turn out okay." Then I should back up my words by being available and willing to help him repair the problem or clean up the mess.

In the Bible, Job's three friends illustrate how difficult it can be to empathize. They sat in silence with Job for seven days, sharing his grief over the disasters that had struck him. When they started talking, things went downhill. They ended up accusing Job of creating his own troubles. It's no wonder Job called them "miserable comforters" (Job 16:2).

Give second chances. In one of my first jobs, I was trying to back a semi-trailer into a tight spot. I thought I was being careful, and in fact, I had gotten out of the truck several times to make sure I wasn't too close to other vehicles. However, I maneuvered too far over without stopping to get out and check, and I hit a car parked nearby. I went inside and found the car's owner, called the boss, and waited unhappily for the police to wrap up the accident report. As you might guess, my boss wasn't pleased, but thankfully he didn't fire me. He gave me a second chance, and I never backed into another vehicle again.

We cannot write someone off the first time they make a mistake or do something we don't like. It is easy to become irritated at someone just because they mispronounce my name or complicate my day. When I remember how many second (and third and fourth) chances I have received, I know I need to pass that grace along to others.

When we first meet someone, we form a quick impression of them. I remember times when my first impression of a new coworker was negative, but later he became a close friend. Likewise, our first impressions of a situation or story we hear are often wrong because we don't have all the information.

There are always several sides to a story, and we probably only have one of them. Blacklisting someone when they mess up is wrong. It's not the way we want to be treated. Giving our coworkers opportunities to make amends when they make mistakes is living out the Golden Rule.

TAKE IT TO WORK

1. How do you like to be treated?
2. Think back to a time when you were sad, discouraged, or upset with yourself. What did you appreciate most from others? How can you pass on that empathy and encouragement to others?
3. Consider how to apply the Golden Rule when a coworker makes a mistake. Think of at least two specific things you could say that show sympathy and support.

Chapter Eighteen

Please Your Boss

We try to get along with our coworkers, but in the end, the most important person for us to get along with may be the boss. After all, if I cannot get along with the boss, I'm likely to quickly find myself without a job!

Perhaps we work in situations where we don't rub shoulders often with our direct superior every day. Even so, we should still aim to please him, and learn to avoid doing things that irritate him. This is not to earn points, but it is simply part of being a good employee.

In some situations you may even have multiple bosses to try to please. And depending on how you look at it, the customer is your boss too.

I hope you have a boss who cares about you as a person, but that is not always the case. Sometimes a manager or foreman is not as interested in getting along with people as much as he is interested in meeting business goals, getting mountains of work completed, or being selfishly served. And though I've always had good employers, I know there are plenty of bad ones out there who are frustrating to work for.

For example, my friend's wife Laurie once worked in customer service for a boss who seemed unreasonable. One time she was on the phone with a customer when her boss also tried to reach her by phone. Laurie stayed on the line with the customer, but her boss told her later to take his calls no matter what. So the next time this happened, she excused herself from a call with a new customer, and took the boss's call. As a result, she lost the customer, who said, "My call must not be important to you."

Laurie was frustrated with these kinds of attitudes coming from the boss, and it wasn't long before she found another job. No matter what kind of boss we have, what are some common-sense things we can do to get along better with them?

1. Know what the boss wants. We should have a clear idea of what we are expected to do. It is difficult to please a person if it is not clear what he wants. This applies to any situation when we are following instructions, even if it is simply a coworker's instructions.

We shouldn't hesitate to ask for clarification or more direction if we are not sure exactly what the boss wants from us in a specific situation. Asking a question doesn't make us look stupid—we look stupid when we do something wrong because we didn't ask for clarification.

It is easier to get on the same page from the beginning than to have to redo something because the boss wasn't pleased. At times I have found myself nodding my head as if I understood what my boss was telling me to do, when I actually was a little confused about it. That's risky. When this happens, instead of nodding, I should stick my neck out and ask for more details.

2. Make your boss's priorities your priorities. What is important to our boss should be important to us. This includes projects, priorities, and time. Our boss's project or priority may not seem important to us, but because it is important to him, it has to become important to us. Even if it is not convenient, we should complete the instructions as soon as we can, and the boss will be pleased.

Sometimes the boss may make a suggestion in passing. I have learned that even though it wasn't an order, if he cared enough to mention it, it was at least subconsciously important to him. When the boss makes a suggestion or asks a question, we should take note of it.

The boss's time is important to him and should be important to us.

One way to respect his time is to make as many decisions on our own as we can. When we do need his input, we can prepare our questions in advance so we can present all the facts quickly. In addition, we should anticipate follow-up questions he may have and be ready to answer them.

3. Deliver what you promise. If we eventually realize that we can't meet our deadline, fulfill our promise, or meet the boss's expectations, we should share the news with him as soon as we can. If we tell him in advance, he won't be surprised and upset to have his plans go awry.

It is much better for our boss to find out from us, than to discover our failure on his own. It is also preferable for him to find out from us, rather than from someone else. We can try to be the first to recognize our failure, own up to it, and then tell our boss how we plan to proceed with correcting the problem.

4. Stay within the authorization the boss has given you. A soldier can be awarded the Medal of Honor for going beyond the call of duty. As employees, going beyond the call of duty is a good thing in many cases, but sometimes it is an effective way to upset the boss.

A person in authority has several options when assigning and delegating tasks. He might ask you to compile some information or prepare a report for him. If he wants your opinion, he might ask what you think he should do in the situation. If he trusts you, perhaps he will even ask you to gather information, make the decision, and let him know what you decided.

As employees, one of our responsibilities is to stay within the bounds of authority the boss has given us. When following instructions and filling our duties, we should be careful we don't stray into territory we haven't been given permission to enter. This includes things like referring questions and decisions to the boss, keeping our mouths shut when we are not to give out information, and not acting in ways that lead others to believe we are more important than we really are.

5. Form strong working relationships. When we are in the middle of a relationship problem or personal dispute at work, we are usually distracted. Instead of focusing on the task at hand, our minds are whirling to process all the nuances of the latest hostile exchange, or we may be praying for help to know how to heal the situation. Depending on the intensity of the conflict, we are stressed out, which wastes time and affects our productivity.

Leaders want their employees to get along. Not only does it hurt productivity, company culture, and morale, it takes up their time because they may need to mediate. If the bad attitudes seep out into the open, customers may even notice. That's a serious problem.

In addition, unhealthy conflict stifles innovation. Creating, refining, and perfecting new ideas into new processes, products, or services takes back-and-forth discussion and debate, critiquing, and "what if" testing.

This critical process can't happen when working relationships are weak. If we dislike our coworkers, we will be either excessively critical of their ideas or extremely defensive of our own. We may be afraid to speak up when we see a weak spot or a problem in the new product or idea.

When we have good working relationships, we can focus on the merits of the idea itself rather than jousting with the person who proposed it. We can feel free to make suggestions for improvement without hurting our coworker's feelings.

As we work to keep a good relationship with our boss, let's remember to look at things from his perspective, care about the same things he cares about, and do what we can to keep his heavy load from getting heavier through our actions.

TAKE IT TO WORK

1. Evaluate your behavior in the workplace. Do you give your boss reason to appreciate you or dislike you? List two ways you can improve.
2. Think of a recent suggestion or comment from your boss, and follow up on it if possible.
3. Observe your coworkers as they relate to their boss. What characteristics seem to improve their interaction? How can you apply the same characteristics?

Chapter Nineteen

Respect Your Coworkers

"Shouldn't you stack those boxes more neatly?" asked Tim.
"Who cares?" Dan said. "It doesn't make any difference."
But when Michael from the warehouse was moving the pallet into storage, the load shifted and some of the boxes fell off. Because Dan didn't do his work carefully, he consistently caused his coworkers extra work. His relationships with them suffered.

Dan should have showed more respect for his coworkers and their time by stacking the boxes more neatly in the first place.

In *Getting Along with People God's Way,* John Coblentz tells of a high school science teacher who would give his students only one rule: the rule of respect. The teacher would say, "If you respect me as teacher, you won't talk out of turn. If you respect each other, you won't fight. If you respect yourself, you won't fight or lie."[11]

Is the rule of respect really that powerful? Imagine what would happen in a workplace if each person respected himself, his coworkers, and the boss. Put respect to work for you with these six principles:

Respect each coworker as a person. Every person has worth. Each person is made in God's image and is a fellow human being. As such, each person deserves respect. One way to respect our coworkers is to treat them as equals regardless of our different positions or skills.

Even if I am a supervisor and my coworker isn't, he is still a person whom God loves. While I may be able to do some things that he cannot, the opposite is also true. He has special gifts and a calling that I do not have.

Have you ever found yourself detesting someone you had trouble getting along with? A simple personality clash can lead to more complicated conflict when we dwell on the issue. Without really intending to, we may start looking down on the other individual as being less of a person than we are. If that happens, we'll probably treat him or her in degrading ways, such as name-calling or contempt. Mocking or manipulating people are other ways we can find ourselves disrespecting other people.

Respect each coworker's abilities and responsibilities. Our coworkers each bring a unique set of experiences and skills to work. They are assigned responsibilities to carry out. Though it may be tempting to jump in and "help" a coworker who we think is not completing his job correctly, this may not be the best approach.

Pushing coworkers aside and doing their jobs for them might be a tempting short-term solution, but it doesn't work over the long-term. It doesn't respect their ability to learn and their responsibility to do their job correctly. I've sometimes fallen into the trap of thinking that my coworkers cannot improve, but that is generally not true.

In addition, sometimes the problem may be only a perceived problem rather than a real one. We may think our own method of getting the job done is better than the method our coworker is using, when in reality, his method may be perfectly acceptable.

Respect each coworker's personal space and belongings. We usually respect others' personal boundaries without really thinking of it. For example, when having a conversation with someone during the workday, we don't stand within two inches of the person. Instead we maintain a respectful distance of a foot or more so we do not invade their personal space.

It can be a little more difficult to respect other personal boundaries at work, but we need to keep them in mind. The principle of Proverbs

25:17 applies here: "Withdraw thy foot from thy neighbour's house; lest he be weary of thee, and so hate thee."

What are some of those personal spaces? In many workplaces, each person has their own work area or desk. Depending on the circumstances, it is best to ask permission before entering the space or using their equipment. For example, if for some reason you need to use a coworker's desk phone, ask for permission first. Or if you would like to use a coworker's coffee maker, ask first if it is okay.

Sometimes we need to borrow our coworkers' tools, equipment, or supplies temporarily. Show respect by treating their tools carefully and returning them to their proper places. It is frustrating when others borrow our things and don't return them, return them broken, or don't return them to the proper place, so we should treat others' tools as well as we do our own.

Respect each coworker's conversations. What is the best thing to do in the following scenario? You have a question, so you go to your coworker to ask him about it. However, you find him in a conversation with another coworker. They continue talking without acknowledging your presence or inviting you to join them. Should you stand by, join the conversation, or edge up closer until they turn to you?

Here's another situation: you overhear your coworker talking on the phone about an issue. The side of the conversation you can hear piques your curiosity and you wonder who she was talking to. When she gets off the phone, should you ask her about it?

Knowing what to do in situations like these isn't always easy. It depends a lot on our relationship with that particular coworker. A good rule of thumb is to keep quiet. We can't go wrong keeping ourselves out of conversations we aren't part of. Neither is it polite to "overhear" your coworker's phone conversation, though you may work so near someone else you can't help it. In that case, the most respectful route is to not say anything about it unless the coworker raises the issue and presents the opportunity to ask.

Respect each coworker's time. Benjamin Franklin said, "Dost thou love life? Then do not squander time, for that's the stuff life is made of." I suppose we all waste time occasionally, but it doesn't make any of us feel good. It feels even worse when *someone else* is wasting our time. We should be conscious of our coworkers' time and not take more of it than they are willing to freely give. They are responsible to make good use of their time because it really belongs to the company.

I sometimes flag down people who are walking past my office. I may have a work-related question for them, or perhaps I'm just taking the opportunity to talk with someone from another part of the building whom I don't often see.

One day I realized that this was probably a bad habit, since I may be wasting my coworkers' time. What if they were on the way to a meeting or appointment or they have a tight schedule that day? My desire to ask the question on the spot could be a sign of my disrespect for their time. Now I try to remember to ask them if they have time to stop for a minute.

Here are some suggestions for respecting our coworkers' time:

- Get to meetings on time.
- Don't take phone calls or allow other distractions while in a work conversation with others.
- Give comprehensive step-by-step instructions up front.
- Take time to reread emails for clarity before sending or replying.
- Take questions and problems to the right person.
- Listen to instructions to get it right the first time.
- Do the job well enough that others don't have to fix our mistakes.
- Write legibly so others don't spend time deciphering the scribbles.

Respect older coworkers' age and experience. I remember one elderly man I worked with years ago. James was slow, hard of hearing, and had bad breath.

Working with older coworkers can be a challenge. Older coworkers tend to look at things differently than the younger generation. They are more likely to be set in their ways and slow to change, and they are often less technologically savvy.

If there is anyone in the workplace who looks at things differently than we do, there is a good chance it's an elderly coworker. Clashes across generations can happen if neither generation respects the outlook of the other.

In *Sticking Points,* a book about generational differences in the workplace, Haydn Shaw uses the analogy of visiting another country. When we travel to a foreign country, we expect their language and food to be different. We adapt to their customs and try to understand the people's history and background. It's an arrogant tourist who expects or demands everything to be the same as back home.[12]

We can use a similar strategy when relating to coworkers from other generations. We don't have to live in the other generation, but when visiting that "country," we can adapt. Though we feel most comfortable in our generation, we can learn to appreciate other generations' ways of thinking and seek to understand reasons for their perspective. Older coworkers can be a real blessing if we let them.

Older coworkers deserve respect for their years of work and experience. If they have been with the company for several decades, they know why things are done the way they are, and save us the trouble of trying something that doesn't work.

Even if they are slower and less technologically savvy than we are, we should respect them for their age and wisdom and look for opportunities to tap into their wealth of experience. Just because their bodies may be slowing down doesn't mean their brains are.

Yes, older coworkers eventually begin to step aside and let someone from the younger generation begin to take more responsibility. When this happens, we should work to make sure our older coworkers don't feel shoved aside, neglected, and unwanted.

Being respectful doesn't just happen—we need to be intentional about it. We can find many more ways to show respect at work than those I have mentioned here. As we practice giving respect to others, we'll find out just how powerful it is.

TAKE IT TO WORK

1. What are specific ways a lack of respect causes inefficiency or problems in your workplace? What are specific ways respect contributes to efficiency and good relationships?
2. Review how you treated your coworkers last week. Did you show respect or disrespect? In what areas should you improve?
3. Identify one coworker to whom you need to show more respect. In what way will you work to show that respect this week?

Chapter Twenty

Stay Calm When Feeling Upset

Kevin stepped up to the group of coworkers circled around his boss on the production floor. "You can't do this," his boss was saying. "Each order needs to go over my desk before you can start." He was visibly upset.

Kevin knew the reason they had gone ahead without the boss's approval was because the boss had been gone that morning. The customer was waiting, and there was nothing else to do but go ahead. The boss wouldn't have been happy if they had sent the customer away empty-handed either.

What would have been the easiest thing for Kevin to do in this situation? Among other things, he could have gotten upset and accused the boss of micro-managing or having poor procedures in place.

Instead, Kevin chose to remain calm and explain the situation. "How would you have liked us to handle this?" he asked. "You were gone, and the customer was waiting."

Kevin's boss is a good example of how losing our temper makes life difficult for people around us. Kevin is a good example of someone keeping his cool in a frustrating situation.

When I'm upset about something, most times I am actually angry. Whether it's coming from a boss, a coworker, or you, anger in the workplace is a problem. Anger almost never helps a situation; I know from hard experience that it makes things worse.

My fourth grade teacher wrote in the "Teacher's Comments" section of my report card, "Concentrate on neatness in your school work. And try not to let games get you upset." I must not have made much progress in this area, because a few years later, after writing "Caleb applies himself well to his studies," my seventh grade teacher added: "He needs to keep working on cheerfully accepting situations not to his liking."

When we are upset or angry, we hurt ourselves and we hurt other people. If we aren't careful, our anger develops into a pattern, which can quickly become a habit that is hard to break. Then we have an even bigger problem on our hands.

How can we learn to see anger as a problem and not a solution? Remembering the following aspects of anger might help.

Anger is an emotion—a strong one. Everyone has emotions, and everyone gets upset. As much as we dislike it when a coworker or boss gets angry at us, we can't just write him off as a "bad boss" because he occasionally gets angry.

God made us emotional people, and He has a purpose for our emotions. Can you imagine an emotionless life? But God does command us to be "slow to wrath" (James 1:19).

Anger must be controlled, just like other emotions. Children often don't do well at controlling their emotions—they may be loudly exuberant or giggly. As adults, we're expected to control our emotions, including our anger. We don't always do so well. The Bible says, "He who is slow to anger is better than the mighty, and he who rules his spirit than he who takes a city" (Proverbs 16:32).

In *War of Words,* Paul David Tripp uses the example of an angry mother yelling at her teenage son to show how we can control ourselves when we really want to. In the middle of the screaming match, the phone rings and the mother answers with a calm, sweet "hello." How is that for control? Why didn't the mother use that same self-control in dealing with her son? This story steps on my toes because I can see myself doing the same thing the mother did.[13]

Anger is usually self-centered. Think about the last time you got angry at work. It was probably over something someone did that you didn't like.

The spark behind anger is generally less than noble. We tend to get angry when things don't go our way, when we feel trapped or helpless, or when we've been humiliated. When we get angry, it is because we are thinking more of ourselves than others.

Anger hurts our relationships at work. Getting angry works against us, not for us. Angry people aren't fun to be around. Even though we would never intentionally hurt our coworkers physically, our angry words can easily hurt their hearts. When that happens, our coworkers will learn to keep their distance. They may or may not avoid us, but certainly they will keep emotionally distant.

Choosing to overlook our coworkers' "transgressions" against us saves our relationships. Proverbs 19:11 says, "The discretion of a man deferreth his anger; and it is his glory to pass over a transgression."

Anger can be destructive. Anger often drives us to action. It sometimes drives us to do things we later regret. Because anger clouds our thinking, sometimes we end up acting in ways and saying things we normally would not.

Getting angry makes situations worse, not better. Even if we don't do physical damage, like throwing a rock, we end up destroying our coworkers' trust in us. We destroy our own reputation.

Anger can be a way to control other people. A person who is habitually angry may eventually begin using it as a way to manipulate other people. Over time, he learns that his coworkers are afraid to do or say certain things around him. He may even enjoy the feeling of control he gets from watching others tiptoe around him. We don't want to become a person like that!

We should never allow ourselves the privilege of throwing a wrench across the shop. When we are upset, remembering that getting angry will only serve to make our problems worse should give us pause. Getting angry isn't worth it.

Proverbs 15:18 says, "A wrathful man stirreth up strife: but he that is slow to anger appeaseth strife." May we be among those who work to ease strife and contention, not those who create it.

TAKE IT TO WORK

1. When was the last time you became upset or angry at work? What was the real reason you were angry? What could you have done differently?
2. Identify situations that tend to make you angry. Determine the best way to react when you recognize one of those situations coming up.
3. Is there a coworker you need to apologize to for being angry?

Chapter Twenty-One

Respond Peaceably to Attacks

I remember picking up my phone at work one day and getting a loud earful. Caught off guard, I was so upset that without thinking I said, "Thanks," and replaced the receiver, cutting off the caller. I immediately regretted my action because I knew I had only made the situation worse.

We don't like being yelled at. It violates the sense of basic decency and respect that should characterize relationships between people. In addition, the other person often catches us off guard and it feels like a surprise attack. The surprise factor combined with feeling threatened triggers a fighting response that almost always escalates the situation.

If you are like me, you often don't respond well to situations like these partly because you don't have time to mentally prepare for them. Our first natural response generally isn't the best response. As writer Ambrose Bierce observed, "Speak when you are angry and you will make the best speech you will ever regret."

Of course, ideally we shouldn't ever have to face attacks or extremely harsh criticism that feels like an attack. If it does happen, what strategies can we learn to keep from making a great speech in a decidedly not-great way? How can we respond peaceably when we feel like we are being attacked?

Slow down. The next time you feel under attack, ask yourself, *Am I being too sensitive or too possessive of my project or idea?* If we are too sensitive, or too attached to a pet project, we might wrongly interpret constructive criticism as an attack. When this happens, we miss opportunities to make the product even better, and we likely damage either our reputation or our relationship, or both.

When we feel under attack, our goal is to respond, not to react. Instead of replying immediately, we could do something else first like take a drink of water or dig out a pad of paper.

Remember that quote from Thomas Jefferson? "When angry, count to ten before you speak. If very angry, count to one hundred." Better advice than counting to ten is simply not to get angry at all, which of course is easier said than done. That is the point of slowing down. Counting to ten helps slow down our response. Proverbs 14:29 says, "He that is slow to wrath is of great understanding: but he that is hasty of spirit exalteth folly."

Even if a person is genuinely upset about a genuine issue, he is in the wrong because he is approaching it the wrong way. If we respond in kind, we are joining him in the wrong. If we can remember this truth, it has a sobering effect on us and helps us reply with "a soft answer."

Intentionally lower your voice. When we feel threatened or attacked, we automatically respond in kind unless we make a conscious decision not to. This means we usually respond forcefully and loudly. As soon as we realize we are literally feeling hot under the collar, we can take that as a reminder to lower our voice.

King Solomon wrote, "A soft answer turneth away wrath: but grievous words stir up anger" (Proverbs 15:1). Speaking quietly helps you keep your cool and helps your coworker control himself also.

Another physical action is to unclench your fists and put your palms up. Try it. Sit down and place your hands, palms up, in your lap. Do you feel more open and vulnerable? When we feel like clenching our firsts under pressure, unclenching them can be a way to relax and reduce physical tension.

Refuse to escalate. Remember that it takes two to fight. If we refuse to "fight back," our coworker has no one to fight with. We should not think of the other person as our enemy. In personal relationship conflicts, it doesn't work to fight fire with fire.

This means sticking to the subject at hand and not bringing in other matters that we could accuse the other person of. His or her problems can be dealt with later by an appropriate person, but the goal at the moment is to get everything calmed down and rational. One way to defuse the situation is to ask, "Could we talk about this tomorrow?" or "May I have a few minutes to think about this?"

Acknowledge the frustration. In any given conflict with a coworker, we may be in the right or we may be in the wrong. In any case, our coworker is upset and we need to respond to that in some way.

Even if we are in the right, we can acknowledge the other's frustration, and if possible, sympathize with it. We can acknowledge that we may have made a mistake or done something that caused a misunderstanding.

Apologize and make an offer. If it is clear that we actually did make a mistake, it's time to apologize for the actions or words that upset our coworker.

Even if we had the best of intentions in our initial action, taking responsibility for what happened may help the other person feel better. We can ask if there is anything we can do to help resolve the situation or fix the problem.

Seek to understand the real source of the problem. Even if the whole unhappy incident is over in a minute, we should look deeper than the words we just heard. Was the issue in question the real issue or was something else driving the whole episode?

The problem that caused our coworker to get angry may not be the real source of the frustration. Perhaps we have unknowingly been irritating him every day for the past week and today he just blew up because he "couldn't take it any longer." This doesn't mean he is justified for his harsh accusations, but at least it helps us understand where he is coming from.

Sometimes criticism can be driven by jealousy. How do I know this? I know this because when I start to feel jealous toward someone, I start to look for his faults. I look for something negative about him, so I can feel better about myself.

It is also possible that our coworker unintentionally overstated his case because he had bottled it up or turned it over in his mind for a while. Suppose you are completely unaware that you have been annoying a coworker for several weeks. Finally one Monday, it all comes out in a big blast.

Instead of feeling attacked, consider that your coworker's comments may have been delivered more forcefully than he intended because he didn't give forethought to the best way to bring up the issue with you.

Seek to bring peace. In *The Peacemaker,* Ken Sande writes about peace-faking, peacemaking, and peace-breaking. Getting even with the other person is an attack response that further breaks the peace. On the other extreme, pretending that the conflict in the relationship doesn't exist is an escape response that is really only faking it. The best option is the middle route of peacemaking, where we seek reconciliation and resolution of the conflict.[14]

One way to bring peace is to go out of our way to be kind and thoughtful even when we feel we are being treated unfairly. First Thessalonians 5:15 teaches, "See that none render evil for evil unto any man; but ever follow that which is good."

In any confrontational situation, our goals of restoring peace and staying in the right should be at the forefront. Our goal should not be to put the other person in his or her place or to defend ourselves.

And if you're wondering what I did after abruptly hanging up the phone the morning I got an earful, I went in person and apologized for being so rude.

TAKE IT TO WORK

1. Observe how other people respond to sudden attacks. Identify which responses bring peace and which responses escalate the conflict. Post a list of the helpful responses where you see it often.
2. Evaluate your attitude toward coworkers who may have accused or become angry at you. Are you holding a grudge or have you forgiven them? Plan to do something for them that will help your attitude and repair the relationship.
3. Do you have any relationships at work where you are peace-faking, simply pretending there is no problem? What should you do about it?

Part Three

Case Studies

Chapter Twenty-Two

Daniel, the Godly Professional

The "background check" turned up nothing. Daniel's 122 colleagues probably combed through files and records; talked to government and business colleagues; checked with reporters, court gossips, and past and present employees; and chased down every possible clue, but still came up empty-handed. Daniel seemed to be completely blameless.

Daniel's coworkers gave up trying to find flaws in his record. "We won't be able to find any fault of his, unless it's concerning the law of his God," they grudgingly concluded.

What a recommendation! What a compliment!

Put yourself in Daniel's shoes. How easy would it be for your coworkers to find incriminating evidence that shows you are not contributing enough time or effort to your job? I know my coworkers could not say, "We won't be able to find any fault in him."

Daniel's life, his accomplishments, and his coworkers' testimony are amazing. Daniel was an outstanding man who led an upstanding life. We know Daniel wasn't perfect, but his dedication and relationship with God resulted in a sterling character. God was able to use him mightily in the workplace. Let's take a closer look at Daniel, a godly professional.

Commitment. Because of his loyalty to God, Daniel has long been lauded as a good example for us. However, his commitment to doing his best for his bosses is no less exemplary.

Daniel must have had a reputation as an excellent worker, for he served in the administration of several different kings. In fact, King Darius was in the process of planning to promote Daniel when the incident of the lions' den occurred.

Selflessness. Though Daniel was an educated and intelligent man who knew what he was doing, the secret of his success as a government official lay in more than just his education. His relationship with his God played a key role.

So it is with us. No matter how experienced or talented we are, our relationship with God is the key to success in getting along with people and doing good work. Who else can help us unselfishly serve customers, deal graciously with coworkers, and control our tempers and tongues when things aren't going well?

Daniel disciplined himself to put God's laws above his own inclinations. He did the same thing at work, where he put the king's interests above his own.

Integrity. Because Daniel served a God who demanded integrity, he didn't fall to the temptations of corruption and vice that commonly trap powerful officials.

Because Daniel's 122 coworkers all seemed to dislike him to the point of actually wanting to see him die, you might think that Daniel is not a good example of someone who was good at getting along with others.

Yet Daniel's integrity may have been a sore spot with the presidents and princes he worked with. It stood as a silent condemnation of their own ungodliness. If they had been upright and honorable men, they would not have plotted against an innocent man as they did.

Daniel's story is a good reminder that even someone who does the right thing and puts effort into getting along with other people won't be able to please everyone. Most of our coworkers' attitudes and feelings are beyond our control.

Inspiration. Daniel's relationship with God gave him access to a higher wisdom than his contemporaries possessed. This became obvious when, of all the king's advisors, only Daniel could interpret certain dreams.

Even beyond these special revelations from God, don't you think God blessed Daniel with wisdom, common sense, and good ideas as he went about his daily work? Like Daniel, we can experience God's blessings on our minds as we work for God's glory and seek His help.

Diplomacy. Even though Daniel's fellow presidents and the princes apparently did not like him, Daniel seemed to be a man who was easy to work with.

Soon after Daniel arrived as a captive in Babylon, he struck a deal with Melzar, the man responsible for the four Hebrew captives. Instead of causing a crisis by refusing to eat the palace provisions, Daniel suggested an alternative—the pulse test.

Surely Daniel approached other potentially problematic issues in his workplace in this same diplomatic manner. Workplace dynamics offer plenty of opportunities to clash, unless we purposefully look for common ground and alternate options as Daniel did.

Humility. Daniel had a lot of successes, but he didn't take credit for them. When he was able to interpret dreams with God's help, he made sure the king knew he had not discovered the dreams' meaning through his own talents. He said, "There is a God in heaven that revealeth secrets . . . But as for me, this secret is not revealed to me for any wisdom that I have more than any living (Daniel 2:28, 30).

Later, in chapter 9 when Daniel prayed to God about the end of the Israelites' captivity, he humbly included himself in his confessions of his people's sins. He uses the pronouns "we," "us," and "our" forty-two times in verses 4 through 18 in chapter 9. "We have sinned, and have committed iniquity," he prayed.

Daniel's humility was part of his success. Like Daniel, we shouldn't feel the need to take credit for or publicize all of our achievements.

Friendship. Further evidence that Daniel was a man of strong relationships comes from King Darius' behavior when he learned he had inadvertently sentenced Daniel to death.

The king's determined efforts to undo the damage he had caused, his night of sleeplessness, his early rising and rush to the lions' den, and the anguish in his voice as he shouted around the stone suggest he was genuinely attached to his top government minister.

As we build connections with our coworkers and even our superiors, hopefully they will become our friends. As our coworkers become our friends, we will enjoy working with them, they will enjoy working with us, and we will each go to greater lengths to keep the relationship working smoothly. We will be willing to go to greater lengths to please each other.

Faithfulness. Not only was Daniel friendly, he was faithful in carrying out his responsibilities at work. His boss was pleased with him, and his coworkers were unable to find any time where he fell down on the job.

Daniel showed his faithfulness to God by praying at his window. That same faithfulness helped him do the right thing in his work, even if it displeased someone else. From the times that Daniel interpreted dreams we know that he was faithful in telling the truth, even when it was bad news for his boss.

Faithfulness is important on the job. Our coworkers, our boss, and our customers suffer when we work with a careless, lackadaisical attitude. Our relationships with these people suffers too.

Attitude. Daniel lived and worked in such a way that everyone could tell he was different. His attitude was different from that of his contemporaries. King Darius noticed that Daniel had "an excellent spirit" (Daniel 5:12).

Once again, this attitude of Daniel's heart was the result of his relationship with God, and it made a difference in his work. That excellent spirit was one reason Darius planned to promote Daniel.

To sum it up, Daniel did his best at work. He did his best to honor God and to get along with his coworkers as well as he could. Though our jobs are far from the high-ranking job Daniel had, when Monday morning comes, we will still benefit if we approach our work and our relationships at work the way Daniel did.

TAKE IT TO WORK

1. Identify areas of your job into which you should put more time and effort. What is hindering you? What must you do to shape up?
2. Consider how your relationships and attitudes at work and your relationship and attitude toward God affect each other. Which is more important? Into which should you put more effort?
3. How often during a regular work week do you seek God's wisdom when confronting problems?

Chapter Twenty-Three

Abraham Lincoln and His Cabinet

What if you thought you were the top candidate and the best person suited for a certain job, and then someone you viewed as a nobody landed the job instead? That is what happened to three prominent politicians in 1860.

As the 1860 Republican presidential nomination convention approached, most people assumed Senator William Seward would be nominated to run for president. Edward Bates, Salmon Chase, and Abraham Lincoln were also in the running, but few people took Lincoln's efforts seriously. In a shock to almost everyone in political circles, the convention voted for Abraham Lincoln as the Republican nominee for president.

The three men who lost the vote—William Seward, Edward Bates, and Salmon Chase—all looked down on Lincoln, and they weren't alone. Unlike many politicians of the day, Lincoln wasn't highly educated, cultured, or experienced in government. He had grown up in a poor family on the frontier and lived in Illinois, which made him a Westerner in the eyes of people on the east coast. Lincoln had served one term in Congress, but since then he had lost two Senate races.

William Seward expressed his feelings this way: "Disappointment! You speak to me of disappointment! To me, who was justly entitled to the Republican nomination for the presidency, and who had to stand aside and see it given to a little Illinois lawyer!"

As we all know, Abraham Lincoln went on to win the presidential election in November 1860. The day after the election, he listed those whom he wanted to be in his Cabinet. Cabinet members are heads of various government departments and serve as advisors to the president. They are a crucial part of government and contribute to a president's success or lack thereof.

Lincoln made his choices thoughtfully. Although Seward, Chase, and Bates had been Lincoln's main opponents, he asked each one to be part of his administration. After much behind-the-scenes wrangling and posturing, eventually each one agreed to serve in the Cabinet of this man they held in low esteem.

Lincoln explained why he had chosen his former rivals: "We needed the strongest men of the party in the Cabinet. We needed to hold our own people together. I had looked the party over and concluded that these were the very strongest men. Then I had no right to deprive the country of their services."

William Seward became Secretary of State, Salmon Chase became Secretary of Treasury, and Edward Bates became Attorney General. Lincoln, while by no means a perfect man, demonstrated much humility and graciousness in relating to these and other men in his day-to-day duties.

Near the end of Lincoln's first term, a discontented and ambitious Salmon Chase tried to gather support for a presidential run against Lincoln. Though Lincoln knew that Chase was plotting against him, he did not try to stop him or demand that Chase leave the Cabinet. He continued to treat Chase with respect and approve appointments Chase made, even though those appointments were Chase supporters.

Though Chase at last unwillingly left the Cabinet in 1864, Lincoln then appointed him to be Chief Justice of the Supreme Court, a powerful position that Chase was eager to have. Lincoln was reluctant to give Chase what he wanted (Lincoln said he would have rather swallowed his buckhorn chair than to appoint Chase), but he thought that Chase was the best man for the job. Lincoln's secretary wrote, "Probably no other man than Lincoln would have had, in this age of the world, the degree of magnanimity to thus forgive and exalt a rival who had so deeply and unjustifiably intrigued against him."

William Seward eventually came to be Lincoln's closest friend and advisor in the Cabinet, and he became personally devoted to Lincoln. When a faction in Congress pressured Lincoln to move Seward out of the Cabinet, Lincoln stood by his appointee, even though Seward offered to resign. Lincoln would often walk to Seward's house to spend the evening with his former rival.

Lincoln seemed to be open to correction and willing to admit his mistakes. A Democrat whom Lincoln had appointed told Lincoln that if he for some reason could no longer support Lincoln, he would resign from his position. Lincoln told him, "That is frank, that is fair. But I want to add one thing: When you see me doing anything that for the good of the country ought not to be done, come and tell me so, and why you think so, and then perhaps you won't have any chance to resign your commission."

Lincoln didn't try to avoid apologizing to those who worked under him. He apologized to a general for a letter he had sent previously. "I was a little cross. I ask pardon." He wrote to another general, "In no case have I intended to censure you, or to question your ability. I frequently make mistakes myself in the many things I am compelled to do hastily." In a letter to General Ulysses Grant, Lincoln confessed that he had doubted one of Grant's battlefield moves. "I now wish to make the personal acknowledgement that you were right, and I was wrong."

In the early years of the Civil War, Lincoln was disappointed when his generals repeatedly allowed the Southern army to escape, preventing a decisive battle from taking place. However, he admitted to a congressman, "I do not know that I could have given any different orders had I been with them myself. I have not fully made up my mind how I should behave when minie-balls were whistling, and those great oblong shells shrieking in my ear. I might run away."

This attitude contrasts with that of Salmon Chase, the Secretary of the

Treasury who hoped to become the next president. Chase said, "So far I have made few mistakes. Indeed, on looking back over the whole ground with an earnest desire to detect error and correct it, I am not able to see where, if I had to do my work all over again, I could in any matter do materially otherwise than I have."

Lincoln showed a forgiving spirit when, a year into the Civil War, he offered Edwin Stanton the powerful post of Secretary of War. He made this choice in spite of Stanton's overt unkindness to him years before. The story goes like this:

Back in the days when Lincoln was an Illinois circuit lawyer, he had been hired by a large Eastern law firm to work on a big legal case that was going to be tried in Chicago. When the trial was moved to Cincinnati, Lincoln's services as a local lawyer were no longer needed. Edwin Stanton was hired instead, but no one told Lincoln. When he arrived in Cincinnati for the trial, Stanton wondered why that "long armed ape" was there and said that Lincoln did not know anything that would contribute to their case.

Stanton expected Lincoln to withdraw from the case, which Lincoln did, although he had worked hard to prepare for it. Even though the two lawyers stayed at the same hotel during the week of arguments, Stanton ignored Lincoln. Surprisingly, Lincoln didn't hold this against Stanton when it came time to choose a new Secretary of War. Throughout the war, Stanton worked closely with Lincoln and came to admire him.

Lincoln stood up for Stanton when Stanton was criticized for not supplying enough troops to a certain general. In a public speech, Lincoln said, "The Secretary of War is not to blame for not giving when he had none to give. I believe he is a brave and able man, and I stand here, as justice requires me to do, to take upon myself what has been charged on the Secretary of War." Listeners applauded.

Because Secretary of War Stanton and President Lincoln respected each other, they worked well together even though they were opposite in many ways. Stanton's secretary wrote, "The secretiveness which Lincoln wholly lacked, Stanton had in marked degree; the charity which Stanton could not feel, coursed from every pore in Lincoln. Lincoln was for giving a wayward subordinate seventy times seven chances to repair his errors; Stanton was for either forcing him to obey or cutting off his head without more ado. Lincoln was as calm and unruffled as the summer sea in moments of great peril; Stanton would lash himself into a fury over the same condition of things. Stanton would take hardships with a groan; Lincoln would find a funny story to fit them. Stanton was all dignity and sternness; Lincoln was all simplicity and good nature."

Once when Stanton disagreed with Lincoln on a relatively minor issue, Lincoln decided not to make an issue of it and let Stanton have his way. He said, "I cannot add to Mr. Stanton's troubles. His position is one of the most difficult in the world . . . The pressure upon him is immeasurable and unending . . . Mr. Stanton is right and I cannot wrongly interfere with him."

Lincoln's patience and forbearance had their limits. In a note to a complaining Major General who had been removed from command, Lincoln wrote, "I have scarcely seen anything from you at any time that did not contain imputations against your superiors. You have constantly urged the idea that you were persecuted because you did not come from West-Point, and you repeat it in these letters. This, my dear general, is I fear, the rock on which you have split."

In a letter to a young captain who was in trouble for speaking disrespectfully to a superior, Lincoln offered these bits of advice: "No man resolved to make the most of himself, can spare time for personal contention. Still less can he afford to take all the consequences, including the vitiating of his temper, and the loss of self-control. Yield larger things to which you can show no more than equal right; and yield lesser ones, though clearly your own. Better give your path to the dog, than be bitten by him in contesting for the right. Even killing the dog would not cure the bite."

As the Civil War drew to a close in 1865, Lincoln's primary concern was to bring the Southern states back into the Union, and he was determined to be as lenient as possible with them.

In his second inaugural address, Lincoln expressed his vision: "With malice toward none, with charity for all, with firmness in the right as God gives us to see the right, let us strive on to finish the work we are in, to bind up the nation's wounds, to care for him who shall have borne the battle and for his widow and his orphan, to do all which may achieve and cherish a just and lasting peace among ourselves and with all nations."

. . . . .

Abraham Lincoln is considered one of the greatest presidents of the United States. This is partly because he was a strong leader during a trying time. But because Lincoln was a man of character, his successes went beyond leading the nation through the war.

Having a top position doesn't give a person permission to just stop getting along with others. It makes the need for good relationships even more important, especially as an example to others.

You and I will never be in the same position Abraham Lincoln was, but we can be inspired by his example of humility and kindness. We can practice the same humility, graciousness, forgiveness, and magnanimity with our coworkers.[15]

TAKE IT TO WORK

1. Do you try to avoid needing to work with people who you perceive to be rivals? Why?
2. Think of some benefits of having a closer working relationship with someone who might be considered your opponent at work.
3. As you practice getting along with others at work, how might that affect other areas of your life, such as family, social, and church life?

Chapter Twenty-Four

Thirty-Three Miners: Coworkers in Deep Trouble

When we leave our jobs at the end of the day and head for home, we are also privileged to be able to leave behind our coworkers. We spend a lot of time with our coworkers, but we get a break from them when we leave work.

But what if you would be trapped with your coworkers in a confined space with your lives on the line? Could you survive? Could you help them survive? Let's take a look at the story of thirty-three coworkers who managed to do just that.

. . . . .

On August 5, 2010, a monster piece of rock, a small mountain itself, broke loose and crashed down through caverns and tunnels deep inside a mountain in Chile.

This was not a normal mountain. For 120 years miners had been digging and blasting inside this mountain, and August 5 was no different. When the miners arrived for work that morning, they had no idea they wouldn't see the light of day for over two months.

The collapse. The only way in and out of the mine was through a large five-mile-long tunnel that spiraled down and down to a depth of over two thousand feet. In some ways this long tunnel, called the Ramp, was similar to a normal road descending a mountain with sharp turns and a steady decline.

The huge dump trucks that hauled rock and ore to the surface could make the trip into the mine in about half an hour. Their return trip, when they were loaded, took them more than an hour. The huge tower of rock that collapsed blocked off several levels of this main road to the top.

Miraculously, no one was killed when this part of the mine collapsed, though some miners suffered relatively minor injuries. But now there was no escape. The shifted piece of the mountain left the miners with no option. There was no way to move it and no way around it.

The thirty-three trapped miners did not know if they would ever be able to get out of the mine. People on the surface had no way of knowing if they had survived the collapsing rock inside the mine. And no one knew if it was even possible to rescue someone that far below the surface. They were at least two thousand feet down. The miners were alive, but buried. Were they living in their own grave?

The first trouble. As the trapped men began to realize the seriousness of their situation, they checked the small food supply in the mine. They found the following:

1 can of salmon
1 can of peaches
1 can of peas
18 cans of tuna
24 liters of condensed milk (8 spoiled)
93 packs of snack cookies

It was clear that unless they conserved and rationed this small amount of food, they would not survive for long. As far as water, plenty of it was available. Though it was dirty, they could drink water from the big tanks of water in the mine for machine use.

It didn't take long for the first trouble to erupt. As some of the miners searched for an escape route in the hours after the accident, a few others raided the food supply against the protest of fellow miners. They ripped open and gobbled up ten packs of cookies.

The rebel ringleaders offered food to other miners who were present, but most of them refused to take any, knowing they weren't authorized to eat. "They only thought of themselves at that moment. They wanted everything. They never thought that we'd be trapped so long," one of those watching said later.

After about two weeks, the men were each eating only a cookie or portion of a cookie every forty-eight hours. They didn't know if they would be found and rescued before they starved to death.

Hope! On the surface, the government organized a rescue effort attempting to find out if the men were alive. Because of the complexity and difficulty of drilling a diagonal shaft that would actually intersect with the mine so deep beneath the surface, nine different drilling rigs were set up to each try to reach the mine.

However, the miners didn't know this. They were starving, and rescue seemed hopeless. As far as they knew, their family and friends assumed they were dead and had already gone back to normal life without them.

Finally, on the evening of the third day underground, the miners were elated to hear the sound of a faraway drill, transmitted through a whole mountain of rock. "What a beautiful noise!" one of the miners shouted. Though the men realized it would be days before a drill could reach them, just knowing that someone was trying to find out whether or not they were still alive brought hope.

Getting along. Around this time, one of the miners wrote in his journal, "We are more relaxed. Down here we're all going to be family. We're brothers and friends because this isn't the kind of thing that can happen to you twice." But reality wasn't always so positive.

Humidity in the mine could reach 98 percent and the temperature could be over 100 degrees. Stuck in a deep, damp, dark, and hot hole in the ground with each other, the thirty-three miners didn't always get along. However, none of the men wanted to be responsible for caring for an injured or bleeding coworker—a cold reality that helped hold back the fist fights that could easily have broken out.

Though the men could hear various drills approaching, all the attempts so far had missed them. They followed the sound of one of the drills all the way to the bottom of the mine and realized that it was headed deeper and deeper into the earth beyond them. It "was like a second death," a miner said. The men couldn't help being depressed.

Once one of the miners lost his temper at one of the older men, accusing him of lying and not knowing what he was talking about. The two men prepared to fight it out. They walked away from the group to settle the matter. Then the one who had started it decided to make peace. He realized they were so close to death already that it didn't make sense to fight. He knew he shouldn't beat up an older man. So instead of fighting, the one who started the argument also ended it; he apologized, and the two men hugged.

Thoughts of God. Being trapped away from their families turned the miners' thoughts toward their families, their past, and their future—and toward God. On the third day after the mine collapse, one of the miners, a man famous for his changing moods, shouted, "I want to pray. I'm angry. I feel powerless." He asked one of the other men to lead in a prayer.

The men knelt, and the prayer began: "We aren't the best men, but Lord, have pity on us." That first prayer meeting became the first of many. The men began meeting each day for prayer, a short sermon, and a time to share their faults and apologize to each other. They knew their predicament was so great only God could get them out of it.

Distractions. The men could still joke with each other though they were slowly starving. One of them called another one "Bicycle Chassis" because he was so thin and bony. Then the nickname was changed to "Butterfly Jerky" because a bicycle chassis was too sturdy to be compared to the hungry miner. In spite of the joke, the truth was that the men were all in poor condition after days of little food and no showers.

To help pass the time, the men made checkers out of cardboard and dominoes out of white plastic pulled off one of the trucks in the mine. Listening to each other tell stories helped take their minds off their troubles.

More hope! The thirty-three miners survived inside the mine for seventeen days before one of the drills broke through into the main tunnel. Elated but also overwhelmed, the miners both celebrated and wept. One of them announced, "God exists." Another one said later, "It felt like a hand had punched through the rock and reached out to us."

The men beat on the drill with a heavy wrench in hopes of the noise being felt or heard by the drill operators. They taped notes to the drill bit. "We are well in the refuge. The 33," one of the notes read.

Bickering. Eventually rescuers sent food and supplies down through the narrow shaft the drill had made. Wires were run, giving the miners phone and video connections to the surface. Far above them the second phase of the rescue began: drilling a hole large enough for a man to fit through.

The miners became famous while they were still underground, as their story was reported across the globe. Their celebrity status brought new pressures and bickering. They dreamed of being rich if they ever made it out. They talked about selling the rights to their story to make a book or film. They heard news that a Chilean millionaire was donating ten thousand dollars to each of them. The millionaire encouraged others to donate money too.

The miners grew suspicious of each other, thinking that some of their group were trying to steal the limelight in order to gain fame and money. For example, a letter that one of the men wrote to his wife claiming to be the absolute leader underground got published in a newspaper. It touched off more relationship problems in the mine when the newspaper was sent into the mine for the men to read.

The miner with the journal wrote, "During the twenty days that we were starving and in despair we were always united, but as soon as the food started arriving and things got a little better, their claws came out and they want to prove who is tougher." He also wrote, "Now that help has arrived, instead of being more united, all we do is fight and argue."

The uncertainty of ever making it out alive added to the mix of emotions in the mine. Now that a supply chain had been established with the surface, the trapped men were living reasonably well, at least compared to what they had endured the first three weeks underground. Yet they still couldn't be certain that the rescue would be successful or that they would make it out of the mine alive. After all, the mountain could collapse again and crush them and their hopes once for all.

Thinking ahead. The miners did eventually see the light of day again.

After thirty-three days of drilling to enlarge the small shaft into a tunnel large enough to lift a man through, the drillers broke through the last bit of rock.

The miners had one last meeting before they took their trips one by one to the surface in a specially designed escape capsule. They worried that a few of the more charismatic and famous of their members would get most of the money from media interviews, books, or other deals.

They agreed that once they were free they would continue to stick together by honoring the decisions of a majority of the group. No one miner could share stories of their grueling time underground. Rather they would share in the telling and in the profits from a book or film about their experiences.

. . . . .

I offer this account not because I expect you to be trapped someday with your coworkers and be forced to get along or die. The story of the miners' grit and endurance is encouraging and offers a fresh perspective on the struggles that I face in my world of work.

Yes, I can find things to complain about in my comfy office job. Yes, I can bicker with my coworkers over issues either trivial or real. In reality, is it worth it?

If I were trapped with my coworkers for sixty-nine days, could we pull together and put up with each other? Compared to what these thirty-three men experienced, getting along with each other at work on an average day seems simple.

Sometime after the rescue, one of the miners told a reporter, "What affected me the most was... seeing my own death, and seeing how my companions were dying, slowly." He added, "You see the capacity of human beings to be sensitive in critical moments, how a kind of love is born, a bond, a brotherhood within a moment of danger."

Our coworkers are real people facing real dilemmas and desires. Let's do our best to help each other at work out of genuine concern.[16]

TAKE IT TO WORK

1. In your relationships with your coworkers, what happens when a crisis occurs?
2. What is one action you can take in stressful situations to keep relationships from being broken?
3. Name two ways you can show your coworkers you recognize and appreciate them as real people.

Appendix

With his knack for humorous writing, Benjamin Franklin wrote four tongue-in-cheek rules for making yourself disagreeable to be around. They all have to do with conversation.

Rules, by the Observation of which, a Man of Wit and Learning may nevertheless make himself a disagreeable Companion.

Your Business is to *shine;* therefore you must by all means prevent the shining of others, for their Brightness may make yours the less distinguish'd. To this End,

1. If possible engross the whole Discourse; and when other Matter fails, talk much of your-self, your Education, your Knowledge, your Circumstances, your Successes in Business, your Victories in Disputes, your own wise Sayings and Observations on particular Occasions, &c. &c. &c.

2. If when you are out of Breath, one of the Company should seize the Opportunity of saying something; watch his Words, and, if possible, find somewhat either in his Sentiment or Expression, immediately to contradict and raise a Dispute upon. Rather than fail, criticise even his Grammar.

3. If another should be saying an indisputably good Thing; either give no Attention to it; or interrupt him; or draw away the Attention of others; or, if you can guess what he would be at, be quick and say it before him; or, if he gets it said, and you perceive the Company pleas'd with it, own it to be a good Thing, and withal remark that it had been said by *Bacon, Locke, Bayle,* or some other eminent Writer; thus you deprive him of the Reputation he might have gain'd by it, and gain some yourself, as you hereby show your great Reading and Memory.

4. When modest Men have been thus treated by you a few times, they will chuse ever after to be silent in your Company; then you may shine on without Fear of a Rival; rallying them at the same time for their Dullness, which will be to you a new Fund of Wit.

Thus you will be sure to please *yourself.* The polite Man aims at pleasing *others,* but you shall go beyond him even in that. A Man can be present only in one Company, but may at the same time be absent in twenty. He can please only where he *is,* you where-ever you are *not.*

End Notes

1   Coblentz, John. *Getting Along with People God's Way* (Christian Light Publications, 2008) pp 10,11 and 35, 36.
2   Lewis, C.S. *Mere Christianity* (HarperCollins Publishers, 2001) p. 121.
3   http://www.law.cornell.edu/cfr/text/14/1214.403
4   Wikipedia article, "Illusory superiority"
5   Wikipedia article, "Dunning-Kruger effect"
6   Kaufman, Josh. *The Personal MBA* (Portfolio/Penguin, 2010) pp. 255-257.
7   Bennett, William J. *Our Sacred Honor* (Simon & Schuster, 1997) pp. 149, 150.
8   Goodwin, Doris Kearns. *Team of Rivals* (Simon & Schuster, 2005) pp. 363, 364.
9   Maxwell, John C. *Winning with People* (Thomas Nelson, 2004) pp. 148, 149.
10 Lencioni, Patrick. *The Three Signs of a Miserable Job* (Jossey-Bass, 2000).
11 Coblentz, John. *Getting Along with People God's Way: A Biblical Study of Interpersonal Relationships* (Christian Light Publications, 2008) p. 51.
12 Shaw, Haydn. *Sticking Points: How to Get 4 Generations Working Together in the 12 Places They Come Apart* (Tyndale House Publishers, 2013) pp 24, 25.
13 Tripp, Paul David. *War of Words* (P&R Publishing, 2000) p. 232.
14 Sande, Ken. *The Peacemaker* (Baker Books, 2004).
15 Information in this chapter compiled from: Goodwin, Doris Kearns. *Team of Rivals* (Simon & Schuster, 2005).
16 Most information in this chapter gleaned from: Tobar, Hector. *Deep Down Dark* (Farrar, Strauss, and Giroux, 2014).

Bibliography

Bennett, William J. *Our Sacred Honor: Words of Advice from the Founders in Stories, Letters, Poems, and Speeches.* New York: Simon & Schuster, 1997.

Coblentz, John. *Getting Along with People God's Way: A Biblical Study of Interpersonal Relationships.* Harrisonburg, VA: Christian Light Publications, 2008.

Goff, Bob. *Love Does: Discover a Secretly Incredible Life in an Ordinary World.* Nashville, TN: Thomas Nelson, 2012.

Goodwin, Doris Kearns. *Team of Rivals: The Political Genius of Abraham Lincoln.* New York: Simon & Schuster, 2005.

Hyatt, Michael. www.michaelhyatt.com. "The Primary Difference Between the Wise and Foolish," "The Quickest Way to Advance Your Career," and various other articles.

Kaufman, Josh. *The Personal MBA: Master the Art of Business.* New York: Portfolio/Penguin, 2010.

Lencioni, Patrick. *The Five Dysfunctions of a Team: A Leadership Fable.* San Francisco: Jossey-Bass, 2002.

Lencioni, Patrick. *The Three Signs of a Miserable Job: A Fable for*

Managers (and Their Employees. San Francisco: Jossey-Bass, 2000.

"Why Great Leadership Fuels Innovation," *Inc.* magazine, December 2014/January 2015 issue.

Lewis, C.S. *Mere Christianity*. New York: HarperCollins Publishers, 2001.

Maxwell, John C. *The 17 Essential Qualities of a Team Player: Becoming the Kind of Person Every Team Wants*. Nashville, TN: Thomas Nelson, 2002.

Winning with People: Discovering the People Principles That Work for You Every Time. Nashville, TN: Thomas Nelson, 2004.

McCullough, David. *John Adams*. New York: Simon & Schuster, 2001.

Miller, John G. *QBQ! The Question Behind the Question: Practicing Personal Accountability in Business and in Life*. Denver, CO: Denver Press, 2001.

Patterson, Kerry, Joseph Grenny, Ron McMillan, and Al Switzler. *Crucial Conversations: Tools for Talking When Stakes Are High*. New York: McGraw Hill, 2012.

Sande, Ken. *The Peacemaker: A Biblical Guide to Resolving Personal Conflict*. Grand Rapids, MI: Baker Books, 2004.

Shaw, Haydn. *Sticking Points: How to Get 4 Generations Working Together in the 12 Places They Come Apart*. Carol Stream, IL: Tyndale House Publishers, 2013.

Standiford, Les. *Meet You in Hell: Andrew Carnegie, Henry Clay Frick, and the bitter partnership that Transformed America*. New York: Crown Publishers, 2005.

Tobar, Hector. *Deep Down Dark*. New York: Farrar, Strauss, and Giroux, 2014.

Tripp, Paul David. *War of Words: Getting to the Heart of Your Communication Struggles*. Phillipsburg, NJ: P&R Publishing, 2000.

www.wikipedia.com, various articles

Acknowledgments

Many different people contributed to this book in various ways, sometimes simply by being part of my life and experience. I especially appreciate those of my family and friends who took interest in my book and blog from the earliest stages. A big thank-you to the following people who were kind enough to review the manuscript, answer questions, and offer suggestions and critiques:

Ken & Jolene Burkholder
Andrew Crider
Nathan Crider
Kyle Crisman
Edwin Eby
Lois Friesen
Steve Galton
Elmer Glick
Samuel & Jodie Heatwole
Merle Herr
Carl Heule
Floyd & Dorcas Miller
Carol Peachey
Jennifer Perfect
Sheila Petre
Weston Showalter
James & Kathryn Swartz
Leon Yoder

Special thanks to Andrew for editing and to Nathan for the "Take It to Work" questions. I am grateful as always for my wife Lois, who freely gave cheerful encouragement, good insight, and wise caution—not to mention blessed shoulder massages as I spent hours hunched over the screen.

And to Marvin at Carlisle Press, thank you for believing in this book and freely sharing your time and insight with me.

I owe everything to God, who changed my life and my relationships, and continues to shape and refine me. I am forever grateful.

About the Author

Caleb Crider lives in Virginia and works for Christian Light Publications. In addition to *Getting Along at Work,* he is the author of *Tell Me the Stories of Jesus,* a beautifully illustrated Bible story book for young children. Caleb is also a freelance writer and editor who helps businesses, organizations, authors, and churches communicate clearly, effectively, and professionally.